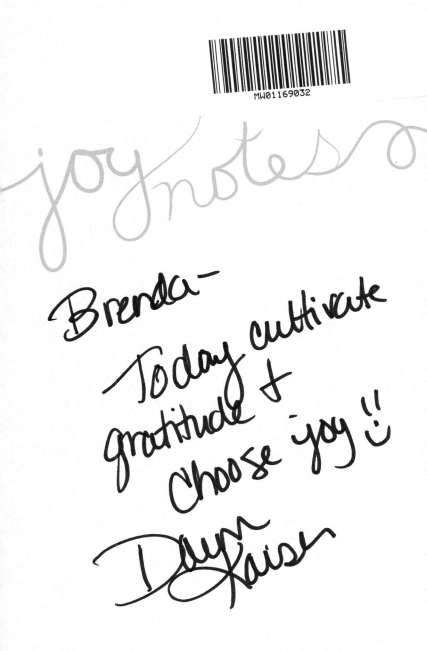

joy notes

Brenda —

Today cultivate
gratitude &
choose joy !!

Dawn Kaiser

302 Sunset Lane
Lake Park, Minnesota 56554

dawnkaiser.com

Edited by Carol McAdoo Rehme.

Cover and interior design by Annette Wood.
annettewoodgraphics.com

Printed in U.S.A.

First Printing, 2015

ISBN 978-0-9967174-0-3

joy notes

BOOK ONE
90 DAYS OF DELIGHT

DAWN KAISER

Dedication

This book is dedicated to the source of all my joy. Thank you, Father God, for making known to me the path of life and speaking through me in all that I say, do and write.

I also want to thank my wonderful friends and family who have brought joy to my heart and helped me experience life to the fullest. I am grateful for your love, support and encouragement on this beautiful journey.

I especially want to thank my mom, my sister and my niece for the smiles they bring to my heart and face. Without your love and support this book would not be a reality.

I am grateful for my editor and designer, who provided insight and ideas to help this book truly connect with the reader.

Introduction

I am a creature of habit, and one habit I developed many years ago was to pick and focus on a single word at the beginning of each year. Admittedly, when I selected a word, I pondered it a few weeks but didn't really reflect on it again until the beginning of the following year. However, in 2014 when I chose the word *joy*—or I should say *joy* chose me—I felt an urge to actually do something with my selection.

As I reflected on *joy*, one of my favorite movies, *The Bucket List*, popped into my head. I recalled the scene of Morgan Freeman and Jack Nicholson sitting in Egypt, gazing at the mysterious pyramids. As they soak up the moment, Morgan says, "The Egyptians believe that when you die, at the entrance of heaven you are asked two questions: First, have you found joy in your life? And second, has your life brought joy to others?"

I ruminated over those two questions and decided to embark on a journey to discover what joy was, where it came from, why so many people might answer "no" to those two questions Morgan posed—and how their answers might be turned into "yes." Because I am an educator at heart, I felt compelled to write about and share what I learned.

Thus, *Joy Notes* evolved.

This book is structured as a devotional journal. I share my thoughts and discoveries about this life-giving word and ask you to reflect and apply *joy* to your life. I would love for you to share how this one word impacts and changes you. Feel free to find me on social media sites and add the hashtag #myjoynote.

> "May the God of hope fill you with all joy and peace
> as you trust in him, so that you may overflow with
> hope by the power of the Holy Spirit."
> Romans 15:13, NIV

"The root of joy is gratefulness."
David Steindl-Rast

We live in a world that constantly reminds us of everything we don't have. We turn on the TV and watch a commercial enticing us to buy the latest and the greatest gadget because without it our lives would not be complete. We open the Sunday newspaper and scan ads trying to convince us we are missing out on the best deals.

Each time we start to focus on what we don't have, our light-heartedness becomes heavier and heavier. The key is to focus on what we do have by practicing an attitude of gratitude.

An attitude of gratitude is more than repeatedly saying you are thankful for your family, your friends and a roof over your head. (Don't get me wrong. You can definitely show appreciation for those godsends.) An attitude of gratitude recognizes all the blessings life holds.

What if I challenge you to list 1,000 things you are grateful for? An impossible task, right? Wrong. The impossible becomes possible by developing a simple habit. Each day write down three things you appreciate. Include big things like getting a brand new car. Include little things like someone holding the door open when you had your hands full.

If you follow this easy task, by this time next year you will have more than 1,000 on your list. You will also have discovered that, by focusing on what you have, you access more joy in your life.

Today, begin to live a life of thankfulness.

I will live with an attitude of gratitude.

My Reflections

After reading today's note, I realize

_____

_____

_____

_____

_____

The key point or phrase I want to remember and practice today is

_____

_____

_____

_____

_____

Today it was easy/difficult for me to experience joy when

_____

_____

_____

_____

Slow Down

> "If we sit with an increasing stillness of the body, and attune our mind to the sky or to the ocean or to the myriad stars at night, or any other indicators of vastness, the mind gradually stills and the heart is filled with quiet joy."
>
> Ravi Ravindra

In the household of my youth, being still equated to being lazy. If you woke on a Saturday morning with plans to just veg, you were sadly mistaken. There was work to be done! Hence, I lived a life focused on *doing* rather than *being*—until I realized we need to do the opposite of what most of us have been taught.

For many years, I believed my joy would increase incrementally as my busyness increased and I checked things off my to-do list. Truth says otherwise: *To have joy flow, we need to go slow.*

Now, that doesn't mean you get to stay in your pajamas and watch reruns of *NCIS* every day. We need to be present and in the moment to absorb all that life has to offer. An old adage advises us to stop and smell the roses.

Today, trade *busyness* for *being* and remember, "Don't hurry. Be happy."

I will slow down and appreciate all that life brings.

My Reflections

After reading today's note, I realize

_____

_____

_____

_____

_____

The key point or phrase I want to remember and practice today is

_____

_____

_____

_____

_____

Today it was easy/difficult for me to experience joy when

_____

_____

_____

_____

joy notes

3
Take Risks

"Take risks. If you win you will be happy. If you lose you will be wise."

Unknown

Yesterday, I watched fourteen young people, including my niece, model courage when they stood before a room full of family, friends and strangers to share their talents. Each of them went out on a limb, daring to sing or play the piano after just a few lessons.

Were they perfect? No. But their joy wasn't founded in perfection; their joy sprang from perseverance and taking a chance.

I know folks who are afraid to do something because they might get sick, they might get hurt or they might fail. When I look into their eyes, I see no spark. To experience all that life has to offer, we must be willing to step out of our comfort zones.

"Dare greatly," says Brené Brown.

We don't have to jump out of an airplane or go zip lining. (Zip lining is pretty cool, though!) Dare to try something new. Dare to do something even when you're timid or frightened.

Deuteronomy 31:6 urges: "Be strong and courageous. Do not be afraid or terrified ... for the Lord your God goes with you; he will never leave you nor forsake you." (NIV)

We don't have to be afraid to take risks because God is bigger than any fear we might hold.

Today, be brave, step out of your comfort zone and watch the magic happen.

I will dare greatly
and try something new.

My Reflections

After reading today's note, I realize

_____

_____

_____

_____

_____

The key point or phrase I want to remember and practice today is

_____

_____

_____

_____

_____

Today it was easy/difficult for me to experience joy when

_____

_____

_____

_____

Trials in Life

> "Count it all joy, my brothers, when you meet trials of various kinds, for you know that the testing of your faith produces steadfastness."
> James 1:1-3, ESV

A friend sent me a note this week, reminding me to count *everything* joy—no matter what. I don't know about you, but when I first read the above scripture I thought, *Obviously, James doesn't know what I am going through.* However, as I began to study the context of the verse, I understood it didn't mean gladness for the situation but rather *hope* for what troubles do in and through me.

The truth is, we will all experience difficult circumstances at one point or another, but our joy is not dependent upon what we are undergoing; rather, it is dependent on what—or whom—we focus during the event.

Instead of asking *why* it happened, we can ask *how* our trial might be used to advance God's cause. We can determine to be stronger coming out of the situation than when we went into it. When we do this, our hope will rise no matter what may come our way.

Today, look at your problem from a new perspective and see the purpose and potential it brings.

I will see the joy in my circumstances.

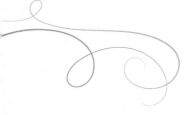

My Reflections

After reading today's note, I realize

_____

_____

_____

_____

_____

The key point or phrase I want to remember and practice today is

_____

_____

_____

_____

_____

Today it was easy/difficult for me to experience joy when

_____

_____

_____

_____

5
Go Out
in Cheerfulness

"For you will go out with joy and be led forth with peace."

Isaiah 55:12, NIV

When you are done getting ready and head to work or an event, how do you go out? Do you go out in anger because your child is throwing a tantrum? Do you go out in anxiety because you are running late, uncertain you will make it on time? Do you go out in misery because all you crave is to crawl back into your pajamas and bed?

We are called to *go out with joy*, to enter into this world with delight and gladness. Not misery and sadness.

One of the most precious hours in our day is right before we leave our houses. What is on your mind during that time? If you watched the news, checked Facebook or rehashed yesterday's problems, you'll find it nearly impossible to feel delight as you face the hours ahead. Fill your mind with uplifting music or read a devotional from this book or spend time listing good things that have happened to you. (And if you can't think of anything, write down in big bold letters, **I AM ALIVE!** Now you've found something to rejoice about.)

Today, be led by peace, calmness and contentment as you journey through the hours ahead.

I will go out in joy.

5
Joy Notes ◎ 10

My Reflections

After reading today's note, I realize

_____

_____

_____

_____

_____

The key point or phrase I want to remember and practice today is

_____

_____

_____

_____

_____

Today it was easy/difficult for me to experience joy when

_____

_____

_____

_____

6
Count Your Blessings

"Man is fond of counting his troubles, but he does not count his joys. If he counted them up as he ought to, he would see that every lot has enough happiness provided for it."

Fyodor Dostoevsky

We have a bad habit of focusing on our problems. When we have coffee with a friend, do many of our conversations begin, "I have to tell you about the most amazing thing that happened to me today"? I'm guessing most start like a conversation in the first episode of television's hit show *Friends*, when Ross conveys he is depressed with the first drawn out "Hi." We start talking about everything that went horribly wrong at work or at home and how we never get a break in life.

We need to disrupt the mode, to talk more about our successes and the good things happening to us. In your next conversation, ask, "What is the best thing that has happened to you today?" Begin to count and share the blessings in your life rather than the problems.

That doesn't mean you can't reach out and ask for help if life has thrown you a curve ball. You won't, however, restore your high spirits by simply being a problem- identifier. Being a problem-solver helps you find contentment in the midst of trial and trouble.

Today, look past your problems
and see what you have received.

I will count my blessings.

My Reflections

After reading today's note, I realize

_____

_____

_____

_____

_____

The key point or phrase I want to remember and practice today is

_____

_____

_____

_____

_____

Today it was easy/difficult for me to experience joy when

_____

_____

_____

_____

7
Rejoice
with Singing

"Where there is salvation there is joy and where there is joy there is singing. They follow one another just as night follows day and day follows night."

Rob Smith

Have you noticed how songs affect your mood?

During college when I was upset that a guy no longer liked me, I always played my Air Supply cassette. (For those who aren't old enough to know, cassettes predated CDs and iTunes.) I never understood why I was more bummed after listening to the songs than when I first began to play them. Eventually, I discovered that when I was in a state of bliss the sound track added to my energy; when I was down, it depressed me. Sad songs, I learned, don't create a happy person.

These days when I'm low, I know exactly which songs to turn to—Matthew West's "Day One" or Mandisa's "Overcomer."

Music is powerful and we were created to sing (even those of us who will never be on "The Voice" or any other musical competition). No matter what we are going through, we are urged to "shout for joy to the LORD, all the earth, burst into jubilant song with music." (Psalm 98:4, NIV)

Today, alter your mood by adjusting your music and letting your soul move to the groove.

I will express my joy
through shouts and song.

My Reflections

After reading today's note, I realize

_____

/ _____

_____

_____

_____

The key point or phrase I want to remember and practice
today is

_____

_____

_____

_____

_____

Today it was easy/difficult for me to experience joy when

_____

_____

_____

_____

8

In the Morning

"Weeping may last through the night, but joy comes in the morning."

Psalm 30:5, NLT

I confess.

I am one of "those people"—people who get up in the morning and are cheerful and happy. I take delight in waking early to watch the sunrise. Now, don't get me wrong. Sunsets are pretty, too, but there is something spectacular about watching the world come to life one brilliant ray at a time.

As I drove to work last week, I was reminded that joy comes to us anew—every day—like the sunrise. Even though there are mornings when I awake to a sun hidden behind clouds, I know it is still there.

The same is true about joy.

Joy may be harder to see sometimes, but it is always there. It is available to us each and every day.

Today, allow your delight to shine—even if there are clouds obscuring your way.

I will let my joy rise anew each day.

My Reflections

After reading today's note, I realize

_____

_____

_____

_____

_____

The key point or phrase I want to remember and practice
today is

_____

_____

_____

_____

_____

Today it was easy/difficult for me to experience joy when

_____

_____

_____

_____

joy notes

9
Change Your
Perspective

"If you change the way you look at things, the things you look at change."

Wayne Dyer

If you ever visit Fargo, North Dakota, don't miss the indoor Ferris wheel at Scheels All Sports store.

I've always like riding Ferris wheels, mainly for the view—a view vastly different than the same sights seen from the ground.

We could all use a Ferris wheel mentality, especially when we are stuck in the muck and mire of daily living. A Ferris wheel mentality helps us surmount the overwhelming struggles of life by changing our perspective. By helping us view our problems from a new angle.

Instead of complaining about how much weight you have to lose, hop onto your mental Ferris wheel and appreciate how many pounds you have already released. Instead of bemoaning the latest gas prices, consider what your days would entail without a car.

You may find life is a whole lot bigger—and brighter—than you thought.

Today, take a ride and see life from a new perspective.

I will change my view
to see the joy in life.

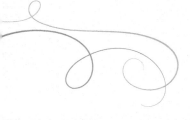

My Reflections

After reading today's note, I realize

_____

_____

_____

_____

_____

The key point or phrase I want to remember and practice today is

_____

_____

_____

_____

_____

Today it was easy/difficult for me to experience joy when

_____

_____

_____

_____

"Everyone has a story to share. Everyone has gone through something that has changed them."
Unknown

Last year, I went to a class called "Writing for Happiness." The instructor discussed how to find bliss in writing. However, so much of what we talked about in class also applied to our lives overall. One particular concept impacted me: Everyone has a story to share; most, however, fear the outcome. They worry about what others think of them.

We base much of our joy on acceptance by others. Yet, if we cannot accept ourselves (or our stories), others won't be able to, either.

Accepting our stories means being content with whom we are and not comparing ourselves to others. It means letting go of labels and judgments, whether inherited or self-inflicted. It means recognizing that *your messes can actually become your messages*, messages to inspire and encourage others.

My sister gave me a sign to hang in my office. It says: "The world is waiting to hear your story."

Today, remember that you have a message to share, to let your voice be heard.

I will share my story.

My Reflections

After reading today's note, I realize

_____

_____

_____

_____

_____

The key point or phrase I want to remember and practice
today is

_____

_____

_____

_____

_____

Today it was easy/difficult for me to experience joy when

_____

_____

_____

_____

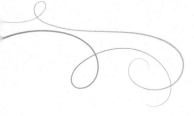

11
Share Your Delight

"Shared joy is double joy and shared sorrow is half sorrow."

Swedish Proverb

How can you set the world on fire with joy? The answer is simple: Share your delight.

When you smile genuinely or write a note of appreciation or simply tell another you are glad to see them, not only are you making a difference to those people, you are also doubling your own gladness.

Try it. It is impossible to *not* feel good when you do something kind for someone else. When you make someone smile or laugh, you lessen the burdens they bear. And, trust me, people tote tons of baggage and brokenness that take a toll on their spirits.

The great thing is, there are oodles of opportunities to share with and care about others. We just have to be open to seeing and seizing the possibilities when they appear. Be creative. (Search YouTube for "Joy Bomb with Aijia," an amazing young woman whose music lifts others.)

Today, focus on seeing and sharing your joy.

I will spread delight to those I meet.

My Reflections

After reading today's note, I realize

_____

_____

_____

_____

_____

The key point or phrase I want to remember and practice today is

_____

_____

_____

_____

_____

Today it was easy/difficult for me to experience joy when

_____

_____

_____

_____

joynotes

Be Joy-full

> *"Everything in your life is a reflection of a choice you* have *made.* If *you* want a different result, make a different choice."
>
> Unknown

You have heard the question, "Are you a half-empty or a half-full kind of person?"

Well, I prefer to ask, "Are you a joy-less or joy-full kind of person?"

Being filled with gladness is less about feeling cheerful and more about living with intention. It is about choosing to find delight in whatever you are doing, whether working, playing, praying, washing dishes .... (Yes, you can find bliss while cleaning a dish!)

I learned early in life to let go of *have to* and replace it with *get to*.

I get to drive to work today.

I get to clean up my messy kitchen.

I get to pay my bills.

Life is about choices. Not all the choices are fun—some are tough—but when I focus on living with purpose, my life overflows with potential and possibility, which leads to more joy.

Today, focus on getting in touch with your soul to make the best choices to live with intention.

I will be a joy-filled person.

My Reflections

After reading today's note, I realize

_____

_____

_____

_____

_____

The key point or phrase I want to remember and practice
today is

_____

_____

_____

_____

_____

Today it was easy/difficult for me to experience joy when

_____

_____

_____

_____

Wear Your Bliss

> "She knew joy was one of her best accessories,
> so she made up her mind to wear it everyday."
> Unknown

I have never been a girl who was into accessorizing.

I might wear a necklace or a bracelet once in a great while, but that's about as far as it goes. Not that I don't like jewelry and other add-ons—I'm just not good at coordinating them with the outfit. Unless accessories are paired with the outfits in store displays, I likely will not put them together myself.

However, when I came across the quote for this Joy Note, I broadened the definition of the word "accessory" to include *joy*—definitely an add-on I can get excited about.

I don't have to worry about colors, patterns or styles. Joy sparkles and shines with any outfit. It complements everything and, when I am wearing it, I feel my best.

Today, make a fashion statement.

I will don joy
before ever leaving the house.

My Reflections

After reading today's note, I realize

_____

_____

_____

_____

_____

The key point or phrase I want to remember and practice today is

_____

_____

_____

_____

_____

Today it was easy/difficult for me to experience joy when

_____

_____

_____

_____

Contagious Contentment

"Be the peace you seek."

Fil Tribble

We talk a lot about viruses. Computer. Influenza. Ebola.

But are you aware that contentment can also be contagious? Contentment means believing you have all you need right now and trusting that there is a Higher Power in control. (And, no, you are not the higher power.) It is about having peace in your heart even though there is a storm outside.

Your composure is not just about you; it infects and affects others as well.

Think about this: Have you ever been around someone who started yawning and, all of a sudden, you yawn, too? Your yawning is less about your need to yawn and more about being influenced to yawn after seeing someone else do it. When life throws you a difficult situation and you remain content, others get curious and take note, desiring to be the same.

Today, spark a revolution of peace and contentment among all those you meet.

I will remain content through my ups and downs.

My Reflections

After reading today's note, I realize

_____

_____

_____

_____

_____

The key point or phrase I want to remember and practice today is

_____

_____

_____

_____

_____

Today it was easy/difficult for me to experience joy when

_____

_____

_____

_____

15
Joy Misplaced

"Your hearts will rejoice and no one will take your joy from you."

John 16:22, ESV

I don't know about you, but I often lose things. Ask my family. There is a running joke in my household: Never buy Dawn expensive gloves because every season she loses several pairs! I'm also frequently hunting for my sunglasses, my cell phone and even my credit cards.

Now, I admit that most of the time these things go missing—not because someone stole them, but because I misplaced them.

I think the same can be said for joy.

No one can steal our cheer. Often, we misplace it by allowing someone or some circumstance to govern our emotions. Some people are garbage trucks of negativity, frustration, anger and disappointment that dump on others. God, however, wants to pour joy into our lives. We choose what we experience and what we share.

Do not allow people or problems to steal from you.

Today, focus on finding the joy you misplaced.

I will not let others rob me of cheer.

My Reflections

After reading today's note, I realize

_____

_____

_____

_____

_____

The key point or phrase I want to remember and practice today is

_____

_____

_____

_____

_____

Today it was easy/difficult for me to experience joy when

_____

_____

_____

_____

"Joy is not in things; it is in us."

Richard Wagner

Have you ever heard someone say, "I will be happy when..."? We live in a society that places hope for happiness on possessions, positions, people and places. Then, when we get those things, we can't figure out why we aren't satisfied.

The problem? We are looking outward when we should be looking inward and upward.

One of my favorite childhood movies was *The Wizard of Oz*. I liked the memorable music and the lovable characters. But as an adult, I see the life lesson Dorothy and her friends were trying to teach us: Your heart, your brain, your courage and your home are all within you. We cannot look to another person, a degree, a badge or a pair of sparkly red shoes to make us feel whole.

The same goes for our joy. We will never find it in things. Joy is in us because God is in us and, like Dorothy and her friends discovered, has been with us all along.

Today, rely on yourself for happiness.

I will find the joy within.

My Reflections

After reading today's note, I realize

_____

_____

_____

_____

_____

The key point or phrase I want to remember and practice
today is

_____

_____

_____

_____

_____

Today it was easy/difficult for me to experience joy when

_____

_____

_____

_____

"I slept and dreamt that life was joy. I awoke and saw that life was service. I acted and behold service was joy."

Rabindranath Tagore

While growing up, I observed my parents actively participating in our community. My dad was a volunteer fireman. He participated in Habitat for Humanity, served on our church council and taught my fourth grade Sunday school class. My mom volunteered her time with the community education program, the church circle and children's ministry. In addition, she coached my summer league softball team.

Not once did I hear them complain about having to serve. They modeled *service as a choice, not a chore*.

When we volunteer (or are volun-*told*), we need to follow Paul's instructions in 2 Corinthians 9:7: "Each of you should give what you have decided in your heart to give, not reluctantly or under compulsion, for God loves a cheerful giver." (NIV)

When we give freely, we get something in return: greater joy for our efforts.

Today, ask how you might give of your time, talent and treasures to bless those in need.

I will serve with gladness.

My Reflections

After reading today's note, I realize

_____

_____

_____

_____

_____

The key point or phrase I want to remember and practice today is

_____

_____

_____

_____

_____

Today it was easy/difficult for me to experience joy when

_____

_____

_____

_____

Foreboding Joy

"Every good and perfect gift is from above, coming down from the Father of the heavenly lights, who does not change like shifting shadows."

James 1:17, NIV

In her book *Daring Greatly,* Brené Brown writes about "foreboding joy," which occurs while we are "waiting for the other shoe to drop" and not allowing ourselves to truly feel delight. We start a new relationship but—fearing it's merely a matter of time before the other person leaves—we hold back. Or, work is going smoothly. Too smoothly. We panic, believing someone is about to pull the rug out from under us.

If we wait expectantly for something to go wrong, we ignore the things that are going right. We need to give ourselves permission to rejoice in all the great things that are happening.

God wants us to enjoy our lives. He showers us with blessings. No matter how often we reject those blessings or expect strings attached, He is waiting and willing to shower us in joy.

Today, delight in the gifts God has given you.

I will receive blessings with open arms.

My Reflections

After reading today's note, I realize

_____

_____

_____

_____

_____

The key point or phrase I want to remember and practice today is

_____

_____

_____

_____

_____

Today it was easy/difficult for me to experience joy when

_____

_____

_____

_____

19
A Fireproof Marriage

"A fireproof marriage doesn't mean that a fire will never come .... But that when it comes, you'll be able to withstand it."

Michael Simmons, *Fireproof*

For the past three weeks, I've listened to a series titled "Happily Even After." In one message, the pastor discussed joy in marriage. He asked a profound question: "Does God use marriage to make us holy more than happy?"

Although I'm not married (yet), I believe God will bring a mate into my life and use our marriage to make us better people. To me, marriage is less about perfection and more about promising to place my spouse's needs ahead of my own. It's about loving each other through the good and the bad.

The other day I told a friend, "I will know the guy I am dating is The One when he's seen me puke and is still willing to be with me!"

Marriage can withstand the tough times. *If* we find joy in the everyday moments. *If* we seek the good in each other. *If* we find room for grace and forgiveness.

Today, dare to love deeply during the good and the bad.

I will focus on the positives in my marriage or relationship!

My Reflections

After reading today's note, I realize

_____

_____

_____

_____

_____

The key point or phrase I want to remember and practice today is

_____

_____

_____

_____

_____

Today it was easy/difficult for me to experience joy when

_____

_____

_____

_____

20
Role Models

"Example is not the main thing in influencing others. It is the only thing."

Albert Schweitzer

Role models demonstrate the way we want to live, act and carry ourselves. We observe their behavior. We try to mimic them. For example, I admire Malala Yousafzai, the youngest Nobel Prize laureate, who fought for equality in education and was courageous in the face of terror.

We should take a closer look at those we admire. Do they live lives of joy even in tough times? Do they respond rather than react to situations? Do they base their decisions on the values they cherish?

Who were your role models and how have they shaped you? Aunt Becky, my mom and grandmother influenced me, giving me a passion for service, a heart for caring and a thirst for reading.

Who are your role models and how are they influencing you? I am blessed to have several inspiring women in my life. One teaches me to be a prayer warrior, another helps me find my uniqueness and yet another models self-love.

Are you a role model and how are you impacting others? Do your admirers see a life of joy or misery? I once scolded my niece for parroting a rude phrase I often used—then realized that would be "the pot calling the kettle black."

Today, adjust your behavior to align with your values.

I will model joy.

My Reflections

After reading today's note, I realize

_____

_____

_____

_____

_____

The key point or phrase I want to remember and practice today is

_____

_____

_____

_____

_____

Today it was easy/difficult for me to experience joy when

_____

_____

_____

_____

Heart Medicine

"A cheerful heart is good medicine, but a broken spirit saps a person's strength."
Proverbs 17:22, NLT

Last year, I decided to tackle an item on my bucket list: Teach a child to roller skate. I took my niece to Skateland, my old elementary school stomping grounds.

The first forty-five minutes were torture. Gracie didn't live up to her name out on the rink. But she didn't give up. Fifty minutes into the lesson, she started catching on.

"Time for one last lap," I said.

Around the final curve, Gracie lost her balance and I couldn't keep mine. In a split second, I had a broken wrist, and within four days I had surgery to repair the shattered bones.

Doctors gave me various medicines to help manage the pain, but I self-prescribed the best medicine of all—a joyful heart. Rather than complain, I focused on gratitude. Although I broke my writing hand, my laptop was equipped with voice recording. I still had the use of my left hand, and my wrist eventually would heal.

Did being cheerful make me heal any faster? Probably not, but it strengthened my spirit. A joyful heart isn't just about loving life when it is perfect; it is about seeing life through the eyes of faith.

Today, administer a healthy dose of positivity.

I will choose to have a cheerful heart.

My Reflections

After reading today's note, I realize

_____

_____

_____

_____

_____

The key point or phrase I want to remember and practice today is

_____

_____

_____

_____

_____

Today it was easy/difficult for me to experience joy when

_____

_____

_____

_____

22
Steps Along
the Journey

"It is good to have an end to journey toward,
but it is the journey that matters in the end."
Ernest Hemingway

Kids are amazing teachers. Just last week, my niece completed her swimming class. To advance to the next level, she had to pass a test. While I sat at the edge of my seat, praying that she'd do the strokes correctly and maintain her buoyancy in the pool, the little fish simply enjoyed the water and the opportunity. Afterward, she wanted to celebrate—at Red Lobster, of course.

Rather than worrying about the next level, Gracie reveled in the journey. What a powerful reminder that joy isn't waiting to be claimed at the final destination. Joy can be discovered along the way. We need to be mindful of each step and take delight in the present.

When we implement a big change in the work world, we stress over it, get it done and—rather than acknowledge our victory—too often we move directly to the next project. Gracie taught that me that we need to celebrate our successes before we step ahead to the next challenge.

Today, celebrate how far you've come.

I will enjoy each step
of this journey called Life.

My Reflections

After reading today's note, I realize

_____

_____

_____

_____

_____

The key point or phrase I want to remember and practice today is

_____

_____

_____

_____

_____

Today it was easy/difficult for me to experience joy when

_____

_____

_____

_____

> "The future belongs to the curious. The ones who are not afraid to try it, explore it, poke at it, question it and turn it inside out."
>
> Unknown

"Why?"

Children ask that question a lot!

Now, I admit this question often seems annoying (and almost defiant), but—for the most part—I believe simple curiosity drives it. Kids are curious creatures. I don't know at what point we seem to lose the urge to ask why, but as I began injecting my life with joy I realized inquisitiveness is a necessity.

Fortunately, there is a wonderful world to discover—if we only think to ask the right questions.

To cultivate curiosity, step outside and turn to nature. You don't have to go on vacation to see the wonders of the world. Go to your backyard or the nearest park or lake.

Watch a sunset. Follow the sweep of a soaring bird. Smell a storm rolling in. You'll feel awakened, refreshed, and alive.

Today, tug on your exploration boots, ask why, look for the answer—and watch your joy bloom.

I will cultivate curiosity.

My Reflections

After reading today's note, I realize

_____

_____

_____

_____

_____

The key point or phrase I want to remember and practice today is

_____

_____

_____

_____

_____

Today it was easy/difficult for me to experience joy when

_____

_____

_____

_____

God's DNA

> "I have told you this so that my joy may be in you and that your joy may be complete."
>
> John 15:11, NIV

In the scientific study of genetics, conversation and controversy center on whether or not doctors can identify certain markers within your DNA to tell how you are made up, who you are and what diseases you might develop later in life.

Essentially, our DNA is the blueprint for our identity.

In addition to physical DNA, we have spiritual DNA. When you accept God into your heart, He places His DNA within you. And God's DNA is spelled J-O-Y!

God is always a part of you, no matter what. Just as it is scientifically impossible to completely remove or dramatically alter our earthly DNA, we cannot erase the imprint of God's DNA from our souls. We forever have His joy within us. It's not dependent on what we do or the results we produce. It is always there.

Today, I will look inward and discover sacred J-O-Y.

I will acknowledge that God's DNA completes me.

My Reflections

After reading today's note, I realize

_____

_____

_____

_____

_____

The key point or phrase I want to remember and practice today is

_____

_____

_____

_____

Today it was easy/difficult for me to experience joy when

_____

_____

_____

_____

25
Focus on
the Present

"The present moment is filled with joy and happiness. If you are attentive, you will see it."
Thich Nhat Hanh

Have you ever collapsed in your bed and wondered where the day went? Or looked at the date on your calendar and realized almost half the year has gone by and you don't know how time passed so quickly?

We rush through life. We have things to do, places to see and people to visit. Too often, we are so busy accomplishing items on our to-do list that we forget to notice and enjoy them.

If we want to experience more joy, we need to focus on the present. When we focus on the past, we feel regretful or sad and when we focus on the future we feel worried and anxious. We need to take delight not only in completing a project or finishing an activity but in doing and experiencing them.

The next time you type a report or cook a dinner, be fully in the moment. Think about how you feel. Listen for the sounds around you. Connect your mind, body and soul.

Today, use your five senses in each activity.

I will live in the _now_.

My Reflections

After reading today's note, I realize

_____

_____

_____

_____

_____

The key point or phrase I want to remember and practice today is

_____

_____

_____

_____

_____

Today it was easy/difficult for me to experience joy when

_____

_____

_____

_____

26
Don't Postpone
Joy

"Don't count the days, make the days count."
Muhammad Ali

More than a decade ago, I got a phone call that changed my life. Mom called to tell my sister and me that Dad had been diagnosed with a terminal brain tumor.

Dad was only forty-eight when God called him to heaven. Even though he died at a young age, he truly lived life to the fullest.

After high school, he entered the Navy's nuclear program, which afforded him opportunities to see the world. He married his high school sweetheart and built their dream house and a family. Most of all, he created a lifetime of memories—some good, some bad. And he enjoyed it all.

Tomorrow doesn't come with a guarantee or a warranty. We can't afford to play the wait-and-see game before we truly start to experience joy. Each day is a gift and we need to unwrap it.

Make a memory. Watch the sunrise. Eat ice cream. Play soccer with your child. Don't postpone joy today for the tomorrow that might not be.

Today, make a memory with someone you love.

I will live life to the fullest each day.

My Reflections

After reading today's note, I realize

_____

_____

_____

_____

_____

The key point or phrase I want to remember and practice today is

_____

_____

_____

_____

_____

Today it was easy/difficult for me to experience joy when

_____

_____

_____

_____

"I cannot even imagine where I would be today were it not for that handful of friends who have given me a heart full of joy. Let's face it; friends make life a lot more fun."

Charles R. Swindoll

I have the privilege of belonging to a wonderful service organization called Altrusa International, which focuses on empowering women and children through education, literacy and leadership. Each year, we hold an "All American Girl Tea Party" where mothers and daughters, grandmothers and granddaughters, aunts and nieces and friends come to share an afternoon of tea to raise money for our projects. As I was working with club members to host this event, I thought about the many friendships I have developed over a coffee or tea conversation.

Someone once said, "Every old friend was once a new friend, so we can't be scared to reach out and make new friends. You never know, they may just become an old friend."

Friendships are a gift from God. I am so grateful for the friends God has brought into my life—some for a season, others for a lifetime.

Find friends who add to your life, not take away from it. Find friends who share your valleys and your victories. You won't regret the effort!

Today, surround yourself with those who bring your heart cheer, not fear.

I will appreciate the gift of friendship.

My Reflections

After reading today's note, I realize

_____

_____

_____

_____

_____

The key point or phrase I want to remember and practice today is

_____

_____

_____

_____

_____

Today it was easy/difficult for me to experience joy when

_____

_____

_____

_____

"Words kill, words give life; they are either poison or fruit—you choose."

Proverbs 18:21, MSG

Words are powerful.

Once said or written—even if recanted, they are etched in the memory of those who heard or read them. Words make a lasting impression, although it might take years before the impact is realized.

We'd be wise to watch how we wield words.

Focus on using words that bring joy. In the movie *Mary Poppins*, the silly-word song "Supercalifragilisticexpialidocious" always makes me smile. I also delight in hearing the word "Auntie"—especially when it's followed by a hug or a smile from my niece.

Another word I love to hear is "hope." God says in Jeremiah 29:11: "For I know the plans I have for you, plans to prosper you and not to harm you, plans to give you hope and a future." (NIV) I don't know about you, but those words definitely fill me with hope.

Speak life to those you meet.

Today, choose words to build rather than tear down.

I will use words to encourage others.

My Reflections

After reading today's note, I realize

_____

_____

_____

_____

_____

The key point or phrase I want to remember and practice
today is

_____

_____

_____

_____

_____

Today it was easy/difficult for me to experience joy when

_____

_____

_____

_____

"May we shout for joy when we hear of your victory and raise a victory banner in the name of our God."

Psalm 20:5, NTL

Do you tend to focus on things that went right or the things that went wrong? Our lives contain peaks and valleys. Peaks are the victorious moments when we achieve success, reach a milestone or meet a goal. Valleys are the lows when we don't get what we're hoping for, aren't chosen or face a loss. It's easy to let disappointment, hurt and pain steal our joy and peace.

A friend challenged me to find a way to hold on to the otherwise fleeting moments of bliss, because they provide energy and feed our faith in the hard times. So I created my Bliss Box. Inside are notes of gratitude and encouragement I receive from clients or friends, little mementos that remind me of the 5K I completed or my first professional job.

Other ideas would achieve the same purpose. How about a Smile File to collect uplifting quotes and stories? What about a Wall of Fame to exhibit certificates, awards and photos?

Whatever method you choose, use it to remember blessings and remind yourself how far you truly have come.

Today, create your personal version of a Bliss Box.

I will celebrate my victories.

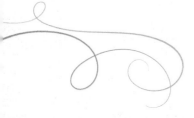

My Reflections

After reading today's note, I realize

_____

_____

_____

_____

_____

The key point or phrase I want to remember and practice today is

_____

_____

_____

_____

_____

Today it was easy/difficult for me to experience joy when

_____

_____

_____

_____

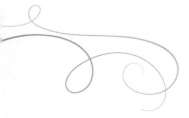

30
Don't Make
Excuses

> "Make the decision that you'll no longer use excuses to keep you from what you know is in your best interest."
>
> Wayne Dyer, *Excuses Begone*

"I'm too busy."

"There is too much stress in my life right now."

"It's too hard."

Excuses roll from our mouths pretty easily these days. No wonder we aren't cultivating gladness. Nike got it right: "Just do it."

One way to let go of excuses is to create a trigger phrase, a switch that alters your attitude. Brook Noel repeats to herself, "Something great is going to happen today and I can't wait to see what it is." Then she's vigilantly alert for those great things— big *and* small.

I use various affirmations to help shift my mentality from excuses to possibilities. I spend five minutes each morning reading these reminders of who I am and how I want to live my life.

Remember the classic children's story, *The Little Engine That Could*? The next time you're tempted to say, "I can't," substitute, "I think I can. I think I can. I think ...."

Today, get out of your own way so something great can happen.

I will let go of excuses.

My Reflections

After reading today's note, I realize

_____

_____

_____

_____

_____

The key point or phrase I want to remember and practice
today is

_____

_____

_____

_____

_____

Today it was easy/difficult for me to experience joy when

_____

_____

_____

_____

31
Inner
Sunshine

"People are like stained-glass windows. They sparkle and shine when the sun is out, but when the darkness sets in; their beauty is revealed only if there is light from within."

Elizabeth Kubler-Ross

I am a sunshine girl. My mood is tied to the sun. When I go outside and soak in its amazing rays, I immediately feel a jolt of energy. And when I haven't been able to see the sun, I feel drained.

The same is true as a Sonshine girl. When I spend time with God, I connect to the life-giving Source of true energy. I can tell when I have let things get in the way of spending time with Him. The good news? No matter the weather outside, the Son shines inside.

Each of us has a light within that needs to be recharged so we can share it. Matthew 5:16 tells us: "Let your light shine before people in such a way that they will see your good actions." (ISV) We cannot do good works on our own and we definitely cannot sustain them for long periods of time without connecting to the Source. We are here to be light and let God shine through our actions.

"There are two ways of spreading light," says Edith Wharton, "to be the candle or the mirror that reflects it."

Today, trade a dark mood for a joyous mood.

I will reflect the Light of the World.

My Reflections

After reading today's note, I realize

_____

_____

_____

_____

_____

The key point or phrase I want to remember and practice
today is

_____

_____

_____

_____

_____

Today it was easy/difficult for me to experience joy when

_____

_____

_____

_____

32
Get Your
Groove On

> "The young women will dance for joy, and the men—old and young—will join in the celebration. I will turn their mourning into joy. I will comfort them and exchange their sorrow for rejoicing."
>
> Jeremiah 31:13, NLT

I am a *Dancing with the Stars* fan. The amateurs make dancing look effortless. Oh, I know they spend über amounts of hours rehearsing, but when they get out on the floor and shake their groove, they make dancing look easy peasy. So much so, that I bought a DVD to learn some moves at home.

Good thing I didn't have a dancing partner, because his feet have been bruised and broken. I will definitely not be getting a "ten from Len" anytime soon!

However, not all dancing has to be focused on doing something correctly or competitively. You can simply move to express your delight. When you are happy, dance. When you are excited, dance. Dancing alters your emotions and physical well-being.

So, if you are feeling blue, get out your dancing shoes and freestyle. There's only one rule: Have fun!

Today, don't worry about holds, foot placement or arms—just let your body move.

I will dance for joy.

My Reflections

After reading today's note, I realize

_____

_____

_____

_____

_____

The key point or phrase I want to remember and practice today is

_____

_____

_____

_____

_____

Today it was easy/difficult for me to experience joy when

_____

_____

_____

_____

"Joy is like oxygen. It is ever present."
Danielle LaPorte

What is the difference between happiness and joy? Personally, I see happiness come and go according to circumstances and the people around me. Rather than being constant, happiness depends on the moment. I can feel happy because something went my way or I can feel unhappy because it didn't.

Joy, on the other hand, is defined as inner delight and contentment despite the outside situation. Joy resides in your heart and mind.

Read what Paul writes in Philippians 4:12: "I know what it is to be in need, and I know what it is to have plenty. I have learned the secret of being content in any and every situation, whether well fed or hungry, whether living in plenty or in want." (NIV) Here is a man who, imprisoned, had every right to moan and groan. Instead, his heart was filled with contentment and gladness—because of the One who filled his heart.

Inward joy is lasting joy. It will not float away like the fleeting and fragile bubbles of happiness.

Today, find Paul's secret for contentment
in any situation.

I will strive for lasting joy.

My Reflections

After reading today's note, I realize

_____

_____

_____

_____

_____

The key point or phrase I want to remember and practice today is

_____

_____

_____

_____

_____

Today it was easy/difficult for me to experience joy when

_____

_____

_____

_____

"Rest is not idleness and to lie sometimes on the grass under trees on a summer's day, listening to the murmur of the water or watching the clouds float across the sky, is by no means a waste of time."

John Lubbock

As kids we played Stop-and-Go. The leader turned his back to the group and yelled, "Go!" When he suddenly turned to face the players and yelled, "Stop!" those who didn't quickly freeze were eliminated from the game.

As an adult, I've often wished some vague leader would turn and yell, "Stop!" because we just keep going, going and going.

Even vacations are exhausting. A few years ago, I went on a Mystery Adventure. The tour guides planned multiple sightseeing excursions between our pick-up and drop-off locations. But my friends and I had a different expectation: rest and relaxation. By the second day, we opted out of the final activity and plopped ourselves on a dock by the lake while the rest of the group carried on.

That was the *best* part of the trip. We sat and talked. We soaked up rays. We refueled our empty tanks.

Don't let life become a game that never ends. Be intentional about down time. Absorb the moment. When you do, you create space for joy to enter.

Remember, "Six days you shall work, but on the seventh day you shall rest. In plowing time and in harvest you shall rest." (Exodus 34:21, ESV)

Today, carve out some R&R for yourself.

I will take time to rest.

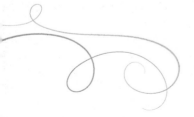

My Reflections

After reading today's note, I realize

_____

_____

_____

_____

_____

The key point or phrase I want to remember and practice
today is

_____

_____

_____

_____

_____

Today it was easy/difficult for me to experience joy when

_____

_____

_____

_____

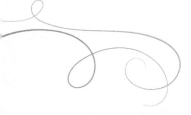

35
Choices

> "One's philosophy is not best expressed in words; it is expressed in the choices one makes ... and the choices we make are ultimately our responsibility."
>
> Eleanor Roosevelt

Each day you are presented with options. What time will you get up? What will you wear? What will you eat? Which route will you drive? Will you smile back at a stranger? Will you work through lunch? The decisions are endless and each impacts your level of joy.

For instance, if I choose to hit the snooze button four times, I will run late and decrease contentment and calmness in my life.

The choices we make are powerful. *They define us, destroy us or develop us.* We are in control. We are empowered to change our minds, to make a different choice if we don't like the outcome we are getting.

We should assess our decisions periodically and be willing to make new ones that help us get closer to where we want to be. I have a friend who quotes the adage: "If it is to be, it is up to me."

Today, carefully evaluate and weigh each decision.

I will make joy-seeking choices.

My Reflections

After reading today's note, I realize

_____

_____

_____

_____

_____

The key point or phrase I want to remember and practice today is

_____

_____

_____

_____

_____

Today it was easy/difficult for me to experience joy when

_____

_____

_____

_____

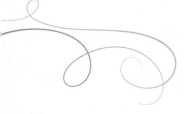

36
Distractions

"One way to boost our will power and focus is to manage our distractions instead of letting them manage us."

Daniel Goleman

"What has happened to all your joy?" Paul asks in Galatians 4:15. I think we might answer, "Uh, dude, things got in the way."

Like the dog in the movie *Up*, we are easily distracted by darting squirrels. Just when we start to focus on experiencing joy, our workload increases or we become consumed with checking social media or we forget to take care of ourselves while we care for others. I am not saying any of those are bad things, but we need to remember that joy doesn't happen only in a carefree or distraction-free life. We need to recognize our shift in focus and redirect it.

The next time there is a shiny object that grabs your attention, acknowledge it, thank God for it and then consider how to use it to create gladness.

Life is flying by. Don't let distractions detour your joy.

Today, turn away from one distraction.

I will overcome the joy detours in my life.

My Reflections

After reading today's note, I realize

_____

_____

_____

_____

_____

The key point or phrase I want to remember and practice today is

_____

_____

_____

_____

_____

Today it was easy/difficult for me to experience joy when

_____

_____

_____

_____

"God is always trying to give blessings to us, but our minds are usually too full to receive them."
Shannon L. Alder

Have you ever given a present and had it rejected?

Maybe someone you know re-gifted something you gave them and you found out. (Hopefully, they didn't re-gift it to you!)

Or maybe they simply handed it back and said, "Thanks, but no thanks."

How rude, you thought.

God has given us many gifts. Yet some of us reject them. We don't even unwrap them before we hand them back. How many times have you talked about needing more patience in life? Perhaps God has given you patience but you haven't yet opened it.

The same is true for joy. In Galatians 5:22, God promises that He has given us all joy here on earth.

Have you opened it?

Today, graciously accept one of His presents that you once rejected.

I will unwrap the gifts God has given me.

My Reflections

After reading today's note, I realize

_____

_____

_____

_____

_____

The key point or phrase I want to remember and practice today is

_____

_____

_____

_____

_____

Today it was easy/difficult for me to experience joy when

_____

_____

_____

_____

Your Thoughts

> "Fix your thoughts on what is true, and honorable, and right, and pure, and lovely, and admirable. Think about things that are excellent and worthy of praise."
>
> Philippians 4:8, NLT

"A penny for your thoughts."

At times, I'm not sure anyone would want to pay for my thoughts because at times they're not worth that much!

I wish I could say that all my thoughts are good and noble; but, honestly, too many are filled with self-doubt and judgment. I have told myself I was not good enough or smart enough or pretty enough. I became a prisoner of my own negative thinking.

To experience absolute joy, we need to let go of the negative and infuse our thoughts with positivity.

Positive thinking isn't like a genie in a bottle—you think it and *poof!* you automatically get it. Rather, our thoughts impact our actions and our actions ultimately impact the life we live.

So if we want more joy, we need to amplify the good in our life in order to drown out the doubt.

Today, give someone your two cents worth—
and make it praise worthy.

I will fix my thoughts on what is
right and pure.

My Reflections

After reading today's note, I realize

_____

_____

_____

_____

_____

The key point or phrase I want to remember and practice today is

_____

_____

_____

_____

_____

Today it was easy/difficult for me to experience joy when

_____

_____

_____

_____

> "Peace does not mean to be in a place where there is no noise, trouble or hard work. It means to be in the midst of those things and still be calm in your heart."
>
> Unknown

Peace and joy are intertwined. Where one goes, the other is sure to follow.

There is a story about a man commissioning two artists to paint a picture of peace. The first painted a meadow with the sun shining, the brook rippling and a bird nesting in the tree—cozy, comfy, calm. The second painted a stormy sea with the clouds darkening, the waves crashing and a bird nesting in the rocks—cozy, comfy, calm.

"Now this," said the man when he saw the stormy artwork, "truly portrays peace!"

Peace isn't a perfect life with all the stars aligned. Peace is serenity even in the midst of chaos.

How much peace do you have? Cultivate calmness by embracing the moment instead of wishing it away. And learn to let go. You heard me right, let go ... and let God.

Today, remain calm in the face of your storm.

I will choose a peace that passes all understanding.

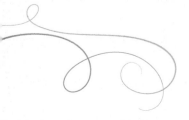

My Reflections

After reading today's note, I realize

_____

_____

_____

_____

_____

The key point or phrase I want to remember and practice today is

_____

_____

_____

_____

_____

Today it was easy/difficult for me to experience joy when

_____

_____

_____

_____

Believe and Live

"What you think or believe only has power when paired with the living of it."

Amy Larsen Davenport

Someone once said, "Joy cannot be found in unbelief."

Do you believe, truly believe, that joy can be experienced in your life?

If you answered, "Yes," do you live what you believe?

Many *claim* to believe in a life of delight, yet they live their days in a state of constant anxiousness, despair or fear. If we really believe in the promise that God came to give us an abundant life (John 10:10) then it should affect how we live.

How do you talk about life? What do you think about your life?

Your lifestyle follows where your mind and mouth lead. We have two choices: We can change our belief or we can change our response to the belief.

Today, listen to see where your mouth leads your mind.

I will live what I believe.

My Reflections

After reading today's note, I realize

_____

_____

_____

_____

_____

The key point or phrase I want to remember and practice today is

_____

_____

_____

_____

_____

Today it was easy/difficult for me to experience joy when

_____

_____

_____

_____

"Life is an echo. What you send out comes back."
Chinese Proverb

Have you ever experienced an echo? Have you shouted or whispered and listened for it to be repeated back to you?

It's important to realize that there are two types of echoes: the echo you hear when you are at the Grand Canyon, and the inner echo that occurs when you think, imagine or do something repeatedly.

Stop and listen. What do you hear? Excuses, complaints and justifications? Or do you hear resounding joy?

Are your echoes filled with faith, hope and love?

Our lives echo our actions. If we want more cheer, we must create more cheer.

Joy is the echo of God's life in us.

Today, "repeat the sounding joy" to echo God.

I will let my life resound.

My Reflections

After reading today's note, I realize

_____

_____

_____

_____

_____

The key point or phrase I want to remember and practice today is

_____

_____

_____

_____

_____

Today it was easy/difficult for me to experience joy when

_____

_____

_____

_____

"Recognize your history, in the present, to know your future."

Helene Lagerberg

Each of us has a past that influences how we live in the present and what we anticipate for the future.

Your joy has a history, too. Some of us keep looking in the rearview mirror and think the present and future look hopeless because of a bad start. But Joyce Meyer reminds us: "You may not have had a good start, but you can have a good finish."

You can trust that God will give you joy in the future—no matter your past—because He always keeps His promises. (Hebrews 10:23, NLT)

Your history is not a prediction of God's future. He wants to shower you with blessings and feed your soul with hope so that you can fully enjoy the present and anticipate the years to come.

Today, create a vision for your future.

I will surrender my past to God.

My Reflections

After reading today's note, I realize

_____

_____

_____

_____

_____

The key point or phrase I want to remember and practice
today is

_____

_____

_____

_____

_____

Today it was easy/difficult for me to experience joy when

_____

_____

_____

_____

43
Smiles

"A cheerful look brings joy to the heart; good news makes for good health."

Proverbs 15:30, NLT

I adore the lyrics Nat King Cole sings: "Smile, though your heart is breaking. Smile, even though it's aching. When there are clouds in the sky, you'll get by. If you smile through your fear and sorrows, smile, and maybe tomorrow you'll see the sun come shining through for you."

Smiles are powerful. In a flash, they elevate my mood. My entire outlook.

How often do you smile? A study in the United Kingdom found that the average adult smiles seven times a day. Eleven times—if she has a more cheerful outlook. Only one time—if she's a grump-on-a-log. Compare those numbers to kids, who smile about four hundred times each day!

Now, I am not a numbers-ninja, but that difference is *huge*. The same study reiterated that a smile really does have the power to transform our day and our mood.

Today, play the smile game and count how many people smile back.

I will elevate my mood to infect the moods of others.

My Reflections

After reading today's note, I realize

_____

_____

_____

_____

_____

The key point or phrase I want to remember and practice today is

_____

_____

_____

_____

_____

Today it was easy/difficult for me to experience joy when

_____

_____

_____

_____

44
Express Yourself

"What you do speaks so loud that I cannot hear what you say."

Ralph Waldo Emerson

One of the classes I teach focuses on communicating with joy. In particular, I discuss how communicating is not about giving information but about getting through to each other. We achieve this through the three V's: verbal, vocal and visual. Out of those three, a study at UCLA found that the breakdown of how we interpret a message from another individual is 7% verbal, 38% vocal, 55% visual—which shows that, when we express ourselves, people pay more attention to our body language than the words we use.

What do your nonverbal cues convey? If I took a picture of your face or your body, what would your expressions portray? Would we see joy, love, kindness, gentleness, patience? Or would we see unhappiness, anger, tenseness, withdrawal?

Today, observe your body language and what it communicates.

I will use gesture and posture to radiate inner joy.

My Reflections

After reading today's note, I realize

_____

_____

_____

_____

_____

The key point or phrase I want to remember and practice today is

_____

_____

_____

_____

_____

Today it was easy/difficult for me to experience joy when

_____

_____

_____

_____

"Everything worth doing starts with being scared."
Art Garfunkel

Have you ever felt fear and joy at the same time? On a first date? The day your baby was born? When you started your new job? Even though you looked forward to the event, you had fears, concerns or doubts.

We talk about exchanging fear to achieve contentment, but Matthew 28:8 reminds us that, rather than being opposites, fear and joy are companions. "So the women hurried away from the tomb, afraid yet filled with joy, and ran to tell his disciples." (NIV) The women were both fearful and joyful. Sharing their glad news was risky.

When we dare to do what God has called us to do, we feel deep satisfaction. Joy comes when we dare to dream even in the face of uncertainty and lack of support. A quote by Robert Schuller hangs on my office wall, asking: "What would you attempt to do if you knew you could not fail?"

So, what *would* you do? Try out for *The Voice*, invite someone to dinner, toss your name in the hat for that promotion? Whatever it is, do it afraid. Don't wait until fear subsides.

Today, dare to dream something significant.

I will take a step forward—
even if I am fearful.

My Reflections

After reading today's note, I realize

_____

_____

_____

_____

_____

The key point or phrase I want to remember and practice today is

_____

_____

_____

_____

_____

Today it was easy/difficult for me to experience joy when

_____

_____

_____

_____

> "Choose a job you love and you will never have
> to work a day in your life."
>
> Confucius

Where do spend most of your waking hours?

If you are like most people, your answer centers on your job. Do you see work as a chore or as a pleasure? Work becomes agreeable when it comes from the heart. Colossians 3:23 reminds us: "Whatever you do, work at it with all your heart, as working for the Lord, not for human masters." (NIV)

We must apply more than our hands and our heads to our assigned jobs. Steve Farber says that heart-driven work is about "doing what you love in the service of people who love what you do."

Do you know what you love? Do you know what you like? Could you list ten answers to each of those questions? I meet people who struggle to give even five answers. We cannot find fulfillment in our work if we don't know what makes our hearts sing.

Today, list your passions and decide how to incorporate them into your life.

I will seek satisfaction in my daily job.

My Reflections

After reading today's note, I realize

_____

_____

_____

_____

_____

The key point or phrase I want to remember and practice today is

_____

_____

_____

_____

_____

Today it was easy/difficult for me to experience joy when

_____

_____

_____

_____

"We do not need magic to transform our world. We carry all of the power we need inside ourselves already."

J.K. Rowling

When I watch a magician, I wonder, *How* did *he do that?* Equally delightful is watching kids watching the same magician. Although I know there is a secret behind his finesse, the kids invariably are in complete awe as items appear and disappear like ... well ... like *magic*!

When do we lose that sense of wonder?

Life is full of miracles and magic, yet oftentimes we are disengaged, bored audience members waiting for something bigger or better to impress us.

There is no sleight-of-hand involved in achieving attitudes of pleasure. We are all promised joy to the fullest (John 15:11). *If we believe, we will receive*.

There is magic all around. We just need to become like children, awed by it all.

Today, seek wonder; wait and watch for magic.

I will refresh and rekindle delight in all things.

My Reflections

After reading today's note, I realize

_____

_____

_____

_____

_____

The key point or phrase I want to remember and practice today is

_____

_____

_____

_____

_____

Today it was easy/difficult for me to experience joy when

_____

_____

_____

_____

> "Make sure that you always follow your heart and your gut, and let yourself be who you want to be, and who you know you are. And don't let anyone steal your joy."
>
> Jonathan Groff

While watching *The Big Bang Theory*, I considered the old debate topic: Which predicts success in life, IQ or EQ? IQ (Intelligence Quotient) measures proficiency in knowledge. EQ (Emotional Quotient) measures self-awareness and empathy for others. On the show, nerdy Sheldon displays IQ, but sorely lacks EQ.

What the television show never addresses is JQ—Joy Quotient. I define JQ as the measurable amount of joy we have and bring to others.

Are you a *bliss buster* or a *bliss builder*? Do you attract delight or repel delight? JQ encompasses all these components—head, heart, hands and gut, enriching our experiences.

We realize true success and deep fulfillment when we live, wholeheartedly, as our true selves—no matter how nerdy or popular we are.

Today, build bliss in a friend or acquaintance.

I will use my JQ to the fullest.

My Reflections

After reading today's note, I realize

_____

_____

_____

_____

_____

The key point or phrase I want to remember and practice today is

_____

_____

_____

_____

_____

Today it was easy/difficult for me to experience joy when

_____

_____

_____

_____

"Be joyful in hope, patient in affliction and faithful in prayer."

Romans 12:13, NIV

Where do you place your hope? Maybe in a relationship, or a job or a success?

We might believe our hopes are well placed, but many times they are *mis*placed. How many times have others disappointed you, not met your expectations? Maybe they promised to help you move but cancelled because "something else came up." Maybe your boss promised things would change at work but nothing did.

John Piper defines hope as "a confident expectation and desire for good that is coming in the future." Our hope is misplaced if we do not set it in the True Source. God is the only One who stays the "same yesterday and today and forever." (Hebrews 13:8, NIV) He will not disappoint us and He always gives us what we need.

Today, shift directions on one of your unmet expectations.

I will place my hope in the One True Source.

My Reflections

After reading today's note, I realize

_____

_____

_____

_____

_____

The key point or phrase I want to remember and practice today is

_____

_____

_____

_____

_____

Today it was easy/difficult for me to experience joy when

_____

_____

_____

_____

Victor Mentality

"For God has not given you a spirit of fear and
timidity, but of power, love and self-discipline."
2 Timothy 1:7, NLT

"It's not my fault."

"Why does this always happen to me?"

"The world is out to get me."

We often hear these comments from people who feel a sense of helplessness or powerlessness and are trying to justify or reason out why their life is the way it is. The blame game, with its victim mentality, impedes the fullness of joy and prevents us from progressing. We must let go of excuses and refuse to let ourselves be conquered.

A victor takes ownership and spends energy looking for ways to change and lessons to take away, writes John Maxwell in his new book, *Sometimes We Win, Sometimes We Learn.* Great leaders approach life with a victor mentality. They focus on the power they have been given. They concentrate on making things happen *because* of themselves rather than allowing things to happen *to* them. They talk about what they can control, what actions they can take and what choices they can make.

Today, choose to be a victor, not a victim.

I will triumph by causing
things to happen.

My Reflections

After reading today's note, I realize

_____

_____

_____

_____

_____

The key point or phrase I want to remember and practice today is

_____

_____

_____

_____

_____

Today it was easy/difficult for me to experience joy when

_____

_____

_____

_____

51
Waiting

"While I'm waiting I will serve you. While I'm waiting I will worship. While I'm waiting I will not faint. I'll be running the race even while I wait."

John Waller

I remember the first time I heard John Waller's song, "While I'm Waiting." I felt like he peeked inside my heart and penned those lyrics just for me. I don't know about you, but it seems like I am always waiting—waiting to grow up, waiting to succeed in my career, waiting to start a family .... I have come to realize that waiting isn't meant to be a punishment or a test. God has reasons why we must sometimes wait.

Maybe He is using this time to draw us closer to Him. As I patiently wait, I grow deeper in my faith walk than I would or could have, had I gotten what I wanted right away.

The next time you are waiting, consider how you might wait contently. Ask, "How can I become the person who is ready to receive what I've been asking for?" Psalm 27:14 states: "Wait on the LORD. Be courageous, and he will strengthen your heart. Wait on the LORD!" (ISV)

Today, believe in the amazing plans God has for you.

I will wait with joy.

My Reflections

After reading today's note, I realize

_____

_____

_____

_____

_____

The key point or phrase I want to remember and practice today is

_____

_____

_____

_____

_____

Today it was easy/difficult for me to experience joy when

_____

_____

_____

_____

"Kindness in words creates confidence. Kindness in thinking creates profoundness. Kindness in giving creates love."

Lao Tzu

Are you down in the dumps today? Maybe you feel like you've been handed lemons and you are tired of drinking lemonade. Do you want to know a way out of your doldrums? Commit a random act of kindness. It's that simple. Showing compassion to others is one of the best ways to experience a joy-filled life.

Write someone a note reminding him of your love. Buy a cup of coffee for a stranger. Leave a big tip for your waitress. I promise you will receive more than you give.

Eight-year-old Alex Mckelvey from Lakewood, Washington, performed 600 acts of kindness between September 2013 and March 2015. She was shooting for sixty. However, once she hit her goal, she didn't want to stop. It's trite but true: Kindness is its own reward.

Today, climb out of your pity-hole and pick someone to serve.

I will perform random acts of kindness.

My Reflections

After reading today's note, I realize

_____

_____

_____

_____

_____

The key point or phrase I want to remember and practice today is

_____

_____

_____

_____

_____

Today it was easy/difficult for me to experience joy when

_____

_____

_____

_____

53
Shouts

> "Those who live at the ends of the earth stand in awe of your wonders. From where the sun rises to where it sets, you inspire shouts of joy."
> Psalm 65:8, NLT

When is the last time you shouted for joy at something God has done to you or through you? Maybe it was a sunset, a cool breeze, a phone call from a friend or a goal He helped you realize. Now when I say shout, I don't mean the thought flitted through your mind or you whispered your glee under your breath or to the person sitting next to you. I mean, when have you shouted so the whole world heard?

SoulPancake asked an audience to shout out their dreams. At first people were timid, but once they started vocalizing their deepest desires, they were able to yell through a megaphone at the top of their lungs!

Don't be afraid to tell others your deepest desires. You never know who might be able to help you make that dream into a reality.

Today, share one of your hidden hopes.

I will shout my dreams to the world.

My Reflections

After reading today's note, I realize

_____

_____

_____

_____

_____

The key point or phrase I want to remember and practice today is

_____

_____

_____

_____

_____

Today it was easy/difficult for me to experience joy when

_____

_____

_____

_____

"Happiness is untested delight, joy is delight tested."

Jack Holes

The question isn't whether life is going to throw you curve balls; rather, when life throws you for a loop, how will you react? When you've been knocked down, no one expects you to jump right up and say, "Let's do that again!" But it's important to understand that inner joy doesn't have to evaporate in the face of trouble.

In 2003 and 2004, I lost several key family members including my dad and my grandmother, pivotal people in my orbit. As I dealt with those losses, I certainly wasn't jumping for joy. I approached each day as it came because that was all that I could handle. I suddenly witnessed the fragility of life and learned not to take for granted that those I love will always be here.

These great losses made me think about the legacy I would leave. My other relationships deepened—all because my inner joy was tested.

I don't wish loss or hard times on anyone, but I do believe that only through trials do we become stronger and able to fully embrace inner peace.

Today, reflect on how the trials of life have made you stronger.

I will seek the lessons hidden in my tests.

My Reflections

After reading today's note, I realize

_____

_____

_____

_____

_____

The key point or phrase I want to remember and practice today is

_____

_____

_____

_____

_____

Today it was easy/difficult for me to experience joy when

_____

_____

_____

_____

55

In the Moment

"It is not how much we have, but how much we enjoy, that makes happiness."

Charles R. Swindoll

Grrrrr.

One of my pet peeves is the people who rush to leave before a concert or show is over. They pay money to attend yet miss the ending because ... who knows? They hope to beat the traffic? Want to press forward with their agenda?

I think we have forgotten how to enjoy the moment we are in. We rush from this to that. We double book ourselves, hoping to sneak out early or sneak in late. And even if our bodies are present, there's no guarantee that our minds are also!

When was the last time you fully attended a conversation or a task without thinking about what you recently did or what is coming down the pipeline? We need to get out of our headspace and into our heartspace. We need to embrace the *now*, take it in, acknowledge it and appreciate it for all it offers.

Don't let the moments pass you by. Don't hold onto the past or fret about the future. Sure, it might take you a bit longer to get out of the parking lot, but that final song could be a life changer.

Today, enjoy each moment.

I will stop rushing through life.

My Reflections

After reading today's note, I realize

_____

_____

_____

_____

_____

The key point or phrase I want to remember and practice today is

_____

_____

_____

_____

_____

Today it was easy/difficult for me to experience joy when

_____

_____

_____

_____

56

Walk by Faith

"Joy is not what we have to acquire in order to experience life in Christ; it is what comes to us when we are walking in the way of faith and obedience."

Eugene Peterson

My friend Bonnie walks by faith. She felt God calling her to coordinate a group to organize Feed My Starving Children in the Fargo, North Dakota area. To do this, she needed to fundraise over $20,000 in one month to purchase and package 100,000 manna packs for children around the world.

It was a bold move. None of them had ever participated in an event of this magnitude. Scarier yet, they had to sign a commitment contract with the international organization.

I wish I could say they made their goal and received a miracle moment, but the truth is the deadline came and the funds fell short. A few weeks later, a local church offered to partner with Bonnie by combining their fundraising efforts. Bonnie agreed. With this joint effort, they provided 200,000 meals, double their original goal!

And it all started with Bonnie's daring deed.

Today, take a leap of faith and do something bold.

I will walk by faith.

My Reflections

After reading today's note, I realize

_____

_____

_____

_____

_____

The key point or phrase I want to remember and practice today is

_____

_____

_____

_____

_____

Today it was easy/difficult for me to experience joy when

_____

_____

_____

_____

"Peace is joy at rest and joy is peace on its feet."
Anne Lamott

Peacekeepers are folks who try to make everyone happy. They don't ruffle any feathers or create conflict. They go with the flow, even when they might have other preferences. They look beyond mere compromise, striving for a win-win.

Romans 12:18 states: "If it is possible, as far as it depends on you live at peace with everyone." (NLT)

This scripture doesn't urge us to be people-pleasers or yes-women. It tells us to be peace*makers*, to focus only on what we can control.

We can promote conciliation by sharing our thoughts, opinions and concerns and listen to all sides with an open mind, allowing others to express their ideas. We can focus on making decisions that promote peace in the world and within ourselves. Peacemakers take an active stand and speak the truth in love.

Today, work diligently at making peace rather than keeping it.

I will maintain an open mind.

My Reflections

After reading today's note, I realize

_____

_____

_____

_____

_____

The key point or phrase I want to remember and practice today is

_____

_____

_____

_____

_____

Today it was easy/difficult for me to experience joy when

_____

_____

_____

_____

58
Set the World
on Fire

"I wanna set the world on fire, until it's burning bright for you. It's everything that I desire; can I be the one you use?"

Britt Nicole

Until 2009, my only international traveling was to Winnipeg, Canada—which might sound like a big deal ... if you didn't know it's only 260 miles from my home. Then, in the flash of a passport, I received an invitation from a pastor that brought the world to my doorstep: I made the decision to take a mission trip to Tanzania, Africa.

The people, the culture, the overwhelming need all captured my heart. I saw poverty and pain. I witnessed strong faith and steadfast hope. I had no idea how I could make a difference, until I remembered the maxim: "To the world you may be one person, but to one person you may be the world."

We all are given gifts to help others.

Today, use your talents to set the world on fire.

I will make a difference.

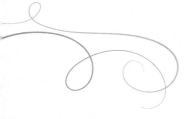

My Reflections

After reading today's note, I realize

_____

_____

_____

_____

_____

The key point or phrase I want to remember and practice today is

_____

_____

_____

_____

_____

Today it was easy/difficult for me to experience joy when

_____

_____

_____

_____

"There are seasons in life. Don't ever let anyone try to deny you the joy of one season because they believe you should stay in another season."
Jane Clayson

Here in Minnesota, we have only two seasons—winter and road construction!

You might think of your life as only two seasons—good and bad. In reality, you get a full range. You might be in grow mode, sow mode, slow mode or flow mode.

Are you learning and growing through situations that are changing you into who you are meant to be? Are you giving and planting, with the intention of leaving the world a better place? Are you on pause, waiting through events that interrupted your plan? Or are you basking in satisfaction as you truly live your purpose?

Seasons come and go with no right or wrong and, sometimes, with no obvious rhyme or reason. But we are told in Ecclesiastes 3:1: "There is a time for everything and a season for every activity under the heavens." (NTL) This includes times of sorrow, times of laughter, times of peace and times of chaos. You may be experiencing a time of pain or brokenness, but as the seasons turn, you will begin to notice beauty and love.

Today, evaluate where you are, your current mode.

I will embrace the seasons of my life.

My Reflections

After reading today's note, I realize

_____

_____

_____

_____

_____

The key point or phrase I want to remember and practice
today is

_____

_____

_____

_____

_____

Today it was easy/difficult for me to experience joy when

_____

_____

_____

_____

60
Endings

> "New beginnings are often disguised as painful endings."
>
> Lao Tzu

Did you know you can find joy in endings?

When an ending occurs, you have a choice. You can choose to see a black abyss that will suck the life out of you, *or* you can see an opportunity for a new beginning.

Joy doesn't always disappear with loss. You might discover it in what is yet to come. Maybe you lost your job; now you have a new opportunity to use your signature strengths. Maybe your relationship has ended; now there's room for the right person to enter your life.

When God closes one door, He always opens another because He wants us to move forward. It's our responsibility to let go of the worry. To hold on to the hope that a new beginning is unfolding. To reflect and look at all the beginnings and endings that led us to this moment. To trust that they will continue.

Endings aren't always easy. But, as Kelly Clarkson sings, "What doesn't kill you makes you stronger."

Today, identify a new beginning that is unfolding.

I will remember that endings lead to a fresh start.

My Reflections

After reading today's note, I realize

_____

_____

_____

_____

_____

The key point or phrase I want to remember and practice today is

_____

_____

_____

_____

_____

Today it was easy/difficult for me to experience joy when

_____

_____

_____

_____

Right Where You Belong

"I've chased a million things, bright lights and empty dreams. Now here I am, right where I thought I wanted to be. I'll trade it all right now, leave it all and lay it down to get back to where I belong."

AJ Michalka

Too often, we get where we wanted to be or get what we wanted to have—only to discover none of it brought us satisfaction or contentment. A profound movie, "Grace Unplugged," reminds me that when I strive to do things on my own, joy is never the end result. Why? Because I do it with the wrong motive in my heart. Or, I try to rush ahead of God because I want it *now*.

We need to do a heart check to see what is really driving our desire. Is it our flesh, our pride, pushing us? Or, do we feel called by God to take action? When I have a strong desire or need, I've learned the best thing to do is to turn it over to God. Ask Him to remove it from my heart if my want doesn't align with His will. And then I wait.

God's timing is perfect and His plan has not gone awry. You are where you belong.

Today, simply let go and let God.

I will trust in God's timing for my life.

My Reflections

After reading today's note, I realize

_____

_____

_____

_____

_____

The key point or phrase I want to remember and practice today is

_____

_____

_____

_____

_____

Today it was easy/difficult for me to experience joy when

_____

_____

_____

_____

> "It is not good for the man to be alone. I will
> make a helper who is just right for him."
>
> Genesis 2:18, NLT

Some days, I think life would be much easier if everyone would just leave ... me ... alone so that I can do my own thing! But we are not meant to go through this world alone. Not that we can't find joy in times of introversion—to read, re-energize or reflect. We all relish those moments. However, one of our most basic human needs is to belong, to be part of something bigger than ourselves.

As part of a community—whether faith-based, service-directed or family-oriented—we receive vital benefits: being cared for, caring for others, better health, strength and delight in togetherness. George Eliot writes: "What greater thing is there for human souls than to feel that they are joined for life—to be with each other in silent unspeakable memories."

When we participate as a community, we create a space to share our victories and our failures. We overcome challenges together that, on our own, would have been impossible. We build a better world.

Today, invest your time and talents in an organization.

I will create space in my schedule
for community.

My Reflections

After reading today's note, I realize

_____

_____

_____

_____

_____

The key point or phrase I want to remember and practice today is

_____

_____

_____

_____

_____

Today it was easy/difficult for me to experience joy when

_____

_____

_____

_____

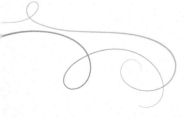

63
Bold Moves

> "Venturing out of your comfort zone may be dangerous, yet do it anyway because our ability to grow is directly proportional to an ability to entertain the uncomfortable."
>
> Twyla Tharp

Picture a chart with two circles. The smaller circle is Your Comfort Zone. The larger circle is Where the Magic Happens. Joy isn't found only in the safe zone. It's also waiting for us when we boldly step out and take a chance.

When Peter saw Jesus walking on water, he could have waited in the safety of the boat with the others. Instead, he said, "If it is really you, call me to come to you out on the water." (Matthew 14:28, MSG) And he jumped out of the boat—without a splash—right on *top* of the water. Peter made a bold move. Imagine the smile stretching across his face as he put one foot in front of the other, a smile of delight—and nervousness—as he literally stepped out of his comfort zone.

We can follow Peter's lead. God tells us over and over again to "fear not." We are designed to take risks, to try new things in spite of being frightened. Even a baby takes a chance with each tottering step.

Let go of *I can't* and *I'll never*. Embrace the possibilities.

Today, step out of your boat.

I will move boldly forward.

My Reflections

After reading today's note, I realize

_____

_____

_____

_____

_____

The key point or phrase I want to remember and practice today is

_____

_____

_____

_____

_____

Today it was easy/difficult for me to experience joy when

_____

_____

_____

_____

Living Your Truth

> "Vulnerability is the birthplace of innovation, creativity and change."
>
> Brené Brown

Are you living your truth every day, or do you hide behind walls and deflectors? Living your truth can be scary because it exposes your vulnerability.

At one time, I equated being vulnerable with weakness and defenselessness, both negative connotations. But when I heard Brené Brown speak, she opened my eyes to wholehearted living. Always striving for perfection (because I believed imperfections were bad), I suddenly realized I wasn't born to be perfect. I was born to be real and whole.

I am not meant to be one person on the outside—projecting confidence, independence and strength—while secretly experiencing doubt, worry and anxiety. My inner and outer lives must balance each other if I hope to live my truth.

Does that mean I must bare my soul to everyone I meet? Absolutely not. But I can let go of my limiting beliefs, show up and let my true self be visible. At the heart of joy-filled experiences in life is vulnerability—when we let our guards down, show courage and are attentive to the moment.

Today, expose an imperfection.

I will live as my true self.

My Reflections

After reading today's note, I realize

_____

_____

_____

_____

_____

The key point or phrase I want to remember and practice today is

_____

_____

_____

_____

_____

Today it was easy/difficult for me to experience joy when

_____

_____

_____

_____

Bucket of Cheer

"The Lord your God will bless you in all your harvest and in all the work of your hands, and your joy will be complete."

Deuteronomy 16:15, NIV

Is your bucket of cheer *depleted* or *completed*? If your bucket is less than full, what is draining it?

Too many times, we let circumstances or people or our jobs zap away our day-to-day pleasure. We need to learn to minimize the zappers and maximize the add-ers. Think about ten things that add joy to your life. How often are those ten things present on a daily basis? How can you make them a consistent part of your routine?

God doesn't promise that life will be easy or smooth sailing, but He does promise complete joy. We just need to do our part by keeping our buckets full.

We also need to become add-ers, helping to fill buckets for others. Helping to refuel their joy.

Today, make time to fill your bucket with something from your List of Ten.

I will scatter cheer.

My Reflections

After reading today's note, I realize

_____

_____

_____

_____

_____

The key point or phrase I want to remember and practice today is

_____

_____

_____

_____

_____

Today it was easy/difficult for me to experience joy when

_____

_____

_____

_____

66
Hide-and-Seek

"For you are my hiding place; you protect me from trouble. You surround me with songs of victory."

Psalm 32:7, NLT

As kids, we spent hours playing Hide-and-Seek. The seeker closed her eyes, counted to ten and started on a quest to find all those who had hidden. A child who found a great place of concealment was jubilant when, one by one, the others were discovered. Eventually, though, the secret spot got … lonely. Was winning worth being alienated from the other kids?

God is the ultimate Seeker. There is no place we can hide from Him. He knows all the best hiding spots. We cannot physically conceal ourselves, nor can we hide our thoughts and emotions from Him. In Psalm 139:2 we read: "You know when I sit down or stand up. You know my thoughts even when I'm far away." (NLT) We don't have to pretend with God. We can be honest and share what we are feeling or thinking. We can tell Him our highs and lows, our joys and our sorrows.

Today, share your heart with Him.

I will not hide from God.

My Reflections

After reading today's note, I realize

_____

_____

_____

_____

_____

The key point or phrase I want to remember and practice today is

_____

_____

_____

_____

_____

Today it was easy/difficult for me to experience joy when

_____

_____

_____

_____

"You have turned my mourning into joyful
dancing. You have taken away my clothes of
mourning and clothed me with joy."
Psalm 30:11, NLT

Are you mindful of what you wear each day? When you go
to your closet, do you choose something comfy and casual
or something dressy and fashionable? (Or maybe you decide
to put on your smarty-pants each day!) We must be equally
thoughtful about our *inner*-wear—our mindsets, our attitudes.

How do you dress your mind? With belief or with doubt?
Love or hate? Humility or pride? Colossians 3:12 says we are
to "dress in the wardrobe God picked out for us: compassion,
kindness, humility, quiet strength and discipline." (MSG) Just like
our regular clothes, we need to put these on—not just once a
day, but every time we interact with another person.

Think how you are clothed on the inside so that when people
ask, "Who are you wearing?" you can answer, "Gifts by God!"

Joy looks good on everyone.

Today, be a trendsetter and pick something new
for your *inner*-wear.

I will choose from God's wardrobe.

My Reflections

After reading today's note, I realize

_____

_____

_____

_____

_____

The key point or phrase I want to remember and practice
today is

_____

_____

_____

_____

_____

Today it was easy/difficult for me to experience joy when

_____

_____

_____

_____

Joy in
the Journey

"Happiness is in heaven, but joy is in the journey."
Unknown

On sunny Sunday afternoons, our family went for leisurely drives along country back roads. Dad drove, Mom rode shotgun, and my sister and I sat in the backseat. There was no particular destination in mind. We were simply together as a family. Mom and Dad sometimes pointed out sights, explained regional history or shared memories of a place or building. The afternoons were peaceful. We simply reveled in the journey.

We need to make our everyday lives more like Sunday drives. We need to slow down, stop going 100 miles an hour. We need to enjoy the ride and take time to soak in and soak up the experience.

If life were mapped out completely, it could be pretty boring. Meaning and memories come from the surprises, the twists and turns and bumps. Gary Allan got it right when he sang: "Life ain't always beautiful, but it's a beautiful ride."

Today, slow down and take in the sights,
sounds and stories.

I will make life an inspiring journey.

My Reflections

After reading today's note, I realize

_____

_____

_____

_____

_____

The key point or phrase I want to remember and practice today is

_____

_____

_____

_____

_____

Today it was easy/difficult for me to experience joy when

_____

_____

_____

_____

"Joy is prayer; joy is strength; joy is love; joy is a net of love by which you can catch souls."
Mother Teresa

On my exploration to learn about joy, I came across the above quote from Mother Teresa. It sums up perfectly what I have discovered so far: Essentially, joy can be broken down into three parts.

Joy as prayer: Sometimes, I feel like an insecure prayer warrior. I start to doubt my words and motives when I pray. But prayer can be more than words; it can be actions. Living with delight acts as a form of prayer.

Joy as strength: We increase our choice muscle every time we experience a valley or a victory. Life is not easy, but we don't have to crumble under the stress. We can make stress our friend and learn to "live strong" no matter what comes our way.

Joy as love: We cannot have gladness without compassion for others. "Love the Lord your God with all your heart and with all your soul and with all your mind and with all your strength. Love your neighbor as yourself. There is no commandment greater than these." (Mark 12:30-31, NIV)

Today, meditate and then activate your love for others.

I will strengthen joy through prayer.

My Reflections

After reading today's note, I realize

_____

_____

_____

_____

_____

The key point or phrase I want to remember and practice today is

_____

_____

_____

_____

_____

Today it was easy/difficult for me to experience joy when

_____

_____

_____

_____

Move Your Body

> "If you don't move your body, your brain thinks you're dead. Movement of the body will not only clear out the sludge, but will also give you more energy."
>
> Sylvia Brown

When is the last time you moved your body? I don't mean getting up from your desk, going to the bathroom and walking back to your chair. (Although that is a start.) When is the last time you moved your body for the pure fun of it? Children know how to make movement playful. While playing Simon Says, they might skip, hop, march, run, jump and hula-hoop!

Movement isn't just for kids. Our bodies were created for action. Research shows the benefits of wiggling, stretching and walking: stronger muscles, increased energy, clearer thinking. Who doesn't want that?

We can do more than run—because, if you are like me, I only run when it's 68 degrees and sunny with a slight breeze (which is why I only run two days out of the year.) We must simply get off the couch and choose something we can move to and that moves us. We can try yoga, piloxing, cycling, dancing or whatever brings a smile. The point is to just ... move.

Today, be like a kid in perpetual, playful motion.

I will jump for pure joy.

My Reflections

After reading today's note, I realize

_____

_____

_____

_____

_____

The key point or phrase I want to remember and practice today is

_____

_____

_____

_____

_____

Today it was easy/difficult for me to experience joy when

_____

_____

_____

_____

"Ask and it will be given to you; seek and you will
find; knock and the door will be opened to you."
Matthew 7:7, NIV

During a shopping excursion, my niece and I passed a toy
display. She boldly asked me to buy her some of the items.

"Let's create a wish list," I suggested. "When your birthday
arrives, I'll pick something from the list and get it for you." Did
I consider her rude for asking? No. She did not throw a fit or
order me. She simply asked.

God wants you to ask for what you need. Maybe not that
brand new BMW or the pricey jewelry you have your eyes on;
those are wants rather than needs. You can, however, ask for
healing, for freedom from temptations, for a door to be opened.
Even so, you might not get the answer you'd hoped.

My dad says, "No one ever died from hearing 'no,' but they
missed opportunities when they weren't courageous enough to
ask in the first place." Ask for what you need. The asking is our
part; the answering is God's part.

Today, ask for something
you've been too timid to request.

I will go to God with my needs.

My Reflections

After reading today's note, I realize

_____

_____

_____

_____

_____

The key point or phrase I want to remember and practice today is

_____

_____

_____

_____

_____

Today it was easy/difficult for me to experience joy when

_____

_____

_____

_____

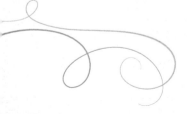

> "We come from the Creator with creativity. I think that each one of us is born with creativity."
> Maya Angelou

"I'm not creative."

"I don't have a creative bone in me."

In spite of what we say, we are all creative beings. However, some of us limit our definition to sculptors, writers, photographers, dancers, musicians or craftsmen—without considering that creativity comes in many forms. Maybe our creativity manifests itself in accounting or building or cooking. Rather than qualify, quantify and compare, we need to let our talents soar.

Creativity is a practiced and disciplined skill. We must work at it. In his book, *Outliers,* Malcolm Gladwell references the 10,000-Hour Rule, which claims that the key to success is practicing a specific skill for a total of 10,000 hours.

How many hours have we practiced?

Today, identify and commit to one talent.

I will dedicate time and attention to honing a skillset.

My Reflections

After reading today's note, I realize

_____

_____

_____

_____

_____

The key point or phrase I want to remember and practice today is

_____

_____

_____

_____

_____

Today it was easy/difficult for me to experience joy when

_____

_____

_____

_____

73

Jump Starts

> "Let your first hour set the theme of success and positive action that is certain to echo through your entire day. Today will never happen again."
> Og Mandino

How do you start and end your day? Do you begin and finish with negativity, stressed because you snoozed too long, stayed up too late or absorbed depressing comments and actions?

Your mind is a vacuum. If you don't purposefully fill it with positivity, it will suck in that vibe most prevalent in our society—negativity.

The first and last hours of each day are important. We need to fill them intentionally. We need to saturate our minds with positivity by seeking God. When our minds are set on Him, we feel energized and empowered to tackle our tasks. Create a bulletin board filled with pictures, quotes and affirmations. Play uplifting music. Count your blessings. Write in your journal. Read your scriptures.

Start and end your day with enriching activities that influence your attitude.

Today, initiate one productive action that will resonate during the hours ahead of you.

I will fill my hours with positivity.

My Reflections

After reading today's note, I realize

_____

_____

_____

_____

_____

The key point or phrase I want to remember and practice today is

_____

_____

_____

_____

_____

Today it was easy/difficult for me to experience joy when

_____

_____

_____

_____

74

Fruit of the Spirit

"A tree is known by its fruit; a man by his deeds. A good deed is never lost; he who sows courtesy reaps friendship, and he who plants kindness gathers love."

Saint Basil

As a kid, I debated with my mother whether a tomato is a fruit or a vegetable. (You probably already know it's a fruit.)

Joy, too, is a fruit. Galatians 5:22-23 states: "The fruit of the Spirit is love, *joy,* peace, patience, kindness, goodness, faithfulness, gentleness and self-control." (ESV) Like a fruit, joy must be grown.

To grow anything, you must plant the seeds in fertile soil, which will allow them to take root. Then you must weed, water and tend. God plants seeds of joy in our hearts and souls; we must weed and fertilize our souls with words and thoughts that nurture those fruits and help them to grow.

Some discover roots forming, a tiny spout pushing through, a bud appearing. Others are already bearing fruit, ripening, coming into season. Wherever you are, at whatever stage of growth, know that the "fruit of the Spirit" is within you.

Today, nurture your joy garden with uplifting thoughts.

I will grow joy in my heart.

My Reflections

After reading today's note, I realize

_____

_____

_____

_____

_____

The key point or phrase I want to remember and practice today is

_____

_____

_____

_____

_____

Today it was easy/difficult for me to experience joy when

_____

_____

_____

_____

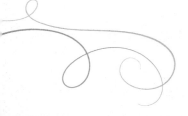

"Delight yourself in the Lord and He will give you the desires of your heart."

Psalm 37:4, NLT

When I started seeking joy, I desired to experience it to the fullest. God definitely delivered, but not always in expected ways. Before this exploration, I never dreamed I would quit my job and strike out on my own. *Maybe someday,* I thought, *but not today.* Through twists and turns, here I am, pursuing my dream of becoming a speaker, writer and coach. And guess what? I have never experienced so much delight.

Is it easy? Absolutely not. But I know God is with me always. I am becoming a woman of faith, and that has been a desire in my heart for many years.

What are the desires of your heart? What are those things you long for in life? Don't limit your focus to what you want to *have*. Stretch yourself. Focus on the person you want to *be*. Focus on how you want to *live*.

Today, pursue your dream.

I will thank God for providing the desires of my heart.

My Reflections

After reading today's note, I realize

_____

_____

_____

_____

_____

The key point or phrase I want to remember and practice today is

_____

_____

_____

_____

_____

Today it was easy/difficult for me to experience joy when

_____

_____

_____

_____

> "Be more concerned with your character than your reputation, because your character is what you really are, while your reputation is merely what others think you are."
>
> John Wooden

There is a difference between personality and character. Personality encompasses our inborn traits. We're introverted or extroverted. We're hardwired to be task-focused or people-focused. Essentially, personality shows in the way we behave publicly.

Character, on the other hand, is formed by perseverance through circumstances. As it says in Romans 5:3-4: "... we know that suffering produces perseverance; perseverance, character; and character, hope." (NLT) Character is the way we behave when no one is watching.

Joy is a character trait we access. We must choose to have it, to build it, to exhibit it each and every day. Delight is inside us, something no one can take. It is not dependent on others, only God.

Today, shape your character by building on joy.

I will push through and persevere.

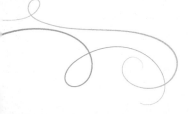

My Reflections

After reading today's note, I realize

_____

_____

_____

_____

_____

The key point or phrase I want to remember and practice today is

_____

_____

_____

_____

_____

Today it was easy/difficult for me to experience joy when

_____

_____

_____

_____

Prayer and Thanks

"Rejoice always; pray without ceasing, in everything give thanks; for this is God's will for you."

1 Thessalonians 5:16-18, NASB

Life is neither perfect nor easy. There are challenges, difficulties and adversities to be faced, but through it all we can don't have to lose hope. To maintain joy through the ashes of adversity, we can follow the instruction given to us in Thessalonians: Pray even though the storms of life are raging.

We know prayer is more than asking for stuff; it includes thanking God for the "stuff" He's given us.

"Thank you, God, that I am going through a divorce." "Thank you for the money problems I am experiencing."

Are you raising your eyebrows? Good.

Look again at the quote above. The verse doesn't say give thanks *for* everything; it says *in* everything give thanks. Even in our darkest hours, we can be thankful for support from family or friends, for resources like counselors, doctors or care facilities, for God who is always by our side even when we don't feel Him there.

Tecumseh, a leader of the Shawnee tribe, said: "When you rise in the morning, give thanks for the light, for your life, for your strength. Give thanks for your food and for the joy of living."

We are to "pray without ceasing." What God brings you to, He will bring you through!

Today, get down on your knees to thank God for seeing you through the difficulties.

I will practice prayer and thanksgiving.

My Reflections

After reading today's note, I realize

_____

_____

_____

_____

_____

The key point or phrase I want to remember and practice today is

_____

_____

_____

_____

_____

Today it was easy/difficult for me to experience joy when

_____

_____

_____

_____

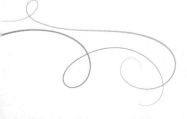

"Since you get more joy out of giving to others,
you should put a good deal of thought into the
happiness that you are able to give."

Eleanor Roosevelt

We all know that it is better to give than to receive. Joy is included! When you give joy, you receive joy—a win-win. Sadly, some don't believe in this principle, focusing instead on getting and holding on tightly to what they have. Theirs is a mentality of scarcity rather than abundance.

We give generously because everything we have is a gift from above. We *get*—to *give*.

Generosity isn't an option. It is a command. Deuteronomy 15:10-11 states: "Give freely and spontaneously. Don't have a stingy heart. The way you handle matters like this triggers God's blessing in everything you do, all your work and ventures. There are always going to be poor and needy people among you. So I command you: Always be generous, open purse and hands, give to your neighbors in a trouble, your poor and hurting neighbors." (MSG)

We are called to help those in need. How might we bring a smile to someone's face or to heal a hurting heart?

Today, be purposeful and aware as you give and receive.

I will freely give of my time,
talent and treasures.

My Reflections

After reading today's note, I realize

_____

_____

_____

_____

_____

The key point or phrase I want to remember and practice today is

_____

_____

_____

_____

_____

Today it was easy/difficult for me to experience joy when

_____

_____

_____

_____

Live out Loud

"When our lives are filled with peace, faith and
joy people will want to know what we have."
David Jeremiah

When people look at your life, what do they see? A person
filled with gladness or sadness? Someone who says one thing
but does another? We are called to be a light unto the world—a
light that shines forth in both word and deed.

Are you positive or negative?

"Oh, I'm a ray of sun shine at work and at home," you say.

What if we ask your family or coworkers to weigh in on the
question? How do they see you?

"She's a ray of sun shine." Or, "She's Eeyore, always bringing
us down every time we start to rise."

We need to make sure our actions and words align. When
I started seminary, a friend advised, "Remember, the best
sermons aren't preached, they are lived out loud."

Today, walk your talk so others will want
to know what you have.

I will live out loud.

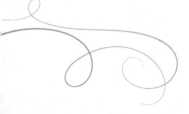

My Reflections

After reading today's note, I realize

_____

_____

_____

_____

_____

The key point or phrase I want to remember and practice today is

_____

_____

_____

_____

_____

Today it was easy/difficult for me to experience joy when

_____

_____

_____

_____

"Hospitality is not about inviting people into our perfect homes; it's all about inviting people into our imperfect hearts."

Unknown

When guests are expected at your house, are you a drill sergeant barking orders, shooting stony stares and stressing out?

Although my family wasn't super messy, when visitors came, our everyday living was not good enough for Mom, who made sure we cleaned every nook and cranny. (Even under the bed and behind the pulled shower curtain. Who looks behind a shower curtain?) Needless to say, I saw hospitality as presenting an *image* instead of sharing our *hearts*.

Until I traveled to Tanzania, Africa, that is.

Villagers welcomed us with smiles and love. They had little, but they gave a lot. The local pastor and his wife moved out of their humble house so we—their mission guests—could move in. (In contrast, I rarely offer my bed, usually providing an inflatable mattress or the couch.) I saw their hospitality as love-in-action. Our comfort was more important than their self-consciousness about their home and possessions.

Hebrews 13:2 counsels: "Do not forget to show hospitality to strangers, for by so doing some people have shown hospitality to angels without knowing it." (NIV)

Today, open your heart and home to someone in need.

I will show hospitality to others.

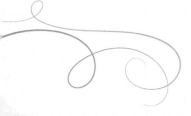

My Reflections

After reading today's note, I realize

_____

_____

_____

_____

_____

The key point or phrase I want to remember and practice today is

_____

_____

_____

_____

_____

Today it was easy/difficult for me to experience joy when

_____

_____

_____

_____

Storms of Life

"Life isn't about waiting for the storm to pass.
It's about learning to dance in the rain."
Vivian Greene

There is no such thing as a problem-free life. Rather than an *if*-a-storm-comes mentality, we'd be wiser to adopt a *when*-the-storm-comes-how-do-we-respond mindset. Do we wait or do we act? Do we give up or push through? Colossians 1:11 says: "You are strengthened with all power according to his glorious might, so that you might patiently endure everything with joy." (ISV)

When trials come, we are to persevere because perseverance builds character.

Successful people weather their storms. Failures, setbacks, breakups ... something tested their characters. They are where they are, they achieved what they achieved, they became who they became—because they pressed on despite the storm.

Today, ignore the thunder and lightning, knowing sunshine will break through the clouds.

I will press forward through rain.

My Reflections

After reading today's note, I realize

_____

_____

_____

_____

_____

The key point or phrase I want to remember and practice
today is

_____

_____

_____

_____

_____

Today it was easy/difficult for me to experience joy when

_____

_____

_____

_____

"Knowing yourself is the beginning of all wisdom."
Aristotle

"Tell me about yourself," someone says.

How do you answer? What do you say? What stories or labels do you use to describe yourself? Are they accurate, or do they reflect what others have said about you?

Disregard your name and job title. Do you know who you are? What makes you smile? What adds energy to your life? What you are passionate about?

To gain understanding and wisdom, we must take time to reflect on how we define ourselves. Proverbs 3:13 states: "Joyful is the person who finds wisdom, the one who gains understanding." (NLT)

You have the power to define yourself, to write your own story. Let go of the labels and opinions and expectations you inherited. Use new descriptors: I am enough; I am content; I am comfortable in my own skin.

Step into your space and own it. Become the person God created you to be.

Today, complete five "I am" statements:

I am _____

I am _____

I am _____

I am _____

I am _____

I will learn to know myself.

My Reflections

After reading today's note, I realize

_____

_____

_____

_____

_____

The key point or phrase I want to remember and practice today is

_____

_____

_____

_____

_____

Today it was easy/difficult for me to experience joy when

_____

_____

_____

_____

Fuel for the Soul

"Faith is a fuel to the engine of soul."
Toba Beta

What happens if you never put gas in your car or you fill it with water? Not only will you not get to your destination, you risk ruining your car.

Yet, this is how we treat our mind and soul. We go, go, go without taking time to refuel. Or, we don't put the right stuff in. We insist on negative self-talk, envy, depression, guilt, hopelessness and helplessness—elements that can't get us to our destination.

We need to tank up with belief, gratitude, positivity, fun and faith!

We need to be aware of our spirit gauge, keeping an eye on it daily, not waiting for "when"—when life slows down, when we're not under pressure, when this troublesome project is done. "When" never actually happens, does it?

When did you last take three long, deep breaths? *When* did you last listen to soul-stirring music? *When* did you last pray or meditate?

Refueling—refreshing and reenergizing—allows room for joy to flow. Don't wait for the check engine light!

Today, breathe and be, to refuel mind and soul.

I will keep my spirit tank full.

My Reflections

After reading today's note, I realize

_____

_____

_____

_____

_____

The key point or phrase I want to remember and practice today is

_____

_____

_____

_____

_____

Today it was easy/difficult for me to experience joy when

_____

_____

_____

_____

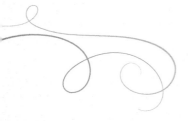

"Faith is taking the first step even when you don't see the whole staircase."
Martin Luther King, Jr.

Someone once said that the saddest summary of life contains three regrets: could have, might have and should have.

I don't want to look back at my life and see a huge list of things I wish had happened; I want a list of things that did happen because I was willing to step out in faith.

In Jeremiah 29:11, we're told that God has good plans for us—if we are willing to let go of the excuses that prevent us from fully receiving His blessings.

When God called Abraham to leave his country and family, he didn't give him all the details. He just said, "Go!" It was up to Abraham to take the first step.

I recently quit my job and started my own business. I didn't have a spouse to support me. I didn't have a plush savings account to carry me through. With amazing friends and family to buoy me, I simply took the step. And God went above and beyond to bless me. Has it been easy? No, but through it all He led the way.

God has a calling for your life, too. Maybe He wants you to volunteer, ask someone out, start a family. Whatever it is, think how you might step forward. Either there will be a staircase or you'll be given wings to fly!

Today, make one move toward your future.

I will take a leap of faith.

My Reflections

After reading today's note, I realize

_____

_____

_____

_____

_____

The key point or phrase I want to remember and practice today is

_____

_____

_____

_____

_____

Today it was easy/difficult for me to experience joy when

_____

_____

_____

_____

One-of-a-Kind

"Today you are you, that's truer than true. There is no one alive who is youer than you."

Dr. Suess

Most of us have envied someone's career, relationships or intelligence. We think, *If I could be more like them, life would be better.*

We need to stop comparing ourselves with others. Comparison robs us of joy. Looking at a friend's present life never tells us what she went through to get there. We admire her successful career without seeing the sacrifices and pain she endured to achieve it.

God didn't make a mistake when He made you. When you pushed from your mother's womb, God didn't look at you and say, "Oops, that one didn't come out as planned." Jeremiah 1:5 states: "Before I formed you in the womb I knew you, before you were born I set you apart; I appointed you as a prophet to the nations." (NIV)

To carry out God's plan for your life, you need to be you. You can't be your coworker or your neighbor or Julia Roberts (unless you *are* Julia Roberts). You are here for a reason.

Today, look in the mirror and verbalize three things that make you one-of-a-kind.

I will cherish my uniqueness.

My Reflections

After reading today's note, I realize

_____

_____

_____

_____

_____

The key point or phrase I want to remember and practice today is

_____

_____

_____

_____

_____

Today it was easy/difficult for me to experience joy when

_____

_____

_____

_____

"For he will order his angels to protect you wherever you go."

Psalm 91:11, NLT

Recently, I received a text message from my niece and her cousin. An attached chalk drawing pictured a man flanked by two angels. One angel, the girls said, was Grandpa Jerry. The other was a family friend who had recently passed. The middle figure was God.

As I looked at the drawing, I thought about Isaiah 41:10: "Don't be afraid, for I am with you. Don't be discouraged, for I am your God. I will strengthen you and help you. I will hold you up with my victorious right hand." (NLT)

Even when we feel lonely, we are never alone. God watches over us and he sends his angels to protect us. When you are driving in your car, God is there. When you are at your desk, God is there. When you are in the doctor's office waiting for a report, God is there.

At my dad's funeral, we played Josh Groban's "To Where You Are"—with lyrics that remind us: "A breath away's not far to where you are." God is only a breath away. He is there whenever and wherever you need Him.

Today, count the number the people who support and cheer you on.

I will let God strengthen and comfort me.

After reading today's note, I realize

_____

_____

_____

_____

_____

The key point or phrase I want to remember and practice today is

_____

_____

_____

_____

_____

Today it was easy/difficult for me to experience joy when

_____

_____

_____

_____

"The greatest gift in life is to be remembered."
Ken Venturi

In the introduction to this book, I mentioned the movie *The Bucket List*. Do you have a bucket list? If so, what does it include? Mine is filled with places I want to visit, experiences I want to have and characteristics I want to cultivate. Now that I think about it, I should call it my Joy List.

A Joy List identifies things that bring you delight, wonderment and fulfillment. It's broader than just *doing* before you die. It includes the legacy you leave behind.

My list originated as the unintentional result of a college writing assignment. The professor asked us to write our own eulogies—with a twist. He told us to look backward from the end (how we wanted to be remembered) to the beginning (how we would get there, or achieve those things).

If we want to be remembered as being giving, how can we start giving *now*? If we want to be remembered as caring, what can we do *now* to show someone we care?

Today, create a Joy List.

I will live my todays with an eye on my final goals.

My Reflections

After reading today's note, I realize

_____

_____

_____

_____

_____

The key point or phrase I want to remember and practice today is

_____

_____

_____

_____

_____

Today it was easy/difficult for me to experience joy when

_____

_____

_____

_____

"Encouragement is oxygen for the soul."
John Maxwell.

In a Work.com survey, only 12% of responders said they receive "frequent appreciation for great work."

It breaks my heart to know people don't feel appreciated. There are so many reasons to acknowledge and thank others. Nobody is perfect, but a little encouragement goes a long way. Encouragement is powerful. It impacts the giver and the receiver.

How often do you like to be told that you don't measure up? I thought not. Yet an inordinate number of our conversations centers on what we need to improve, how we need to change, what we need to fix.

Not that we shouldn't try to grow, but think how different those conversations would sound with, say, an 80/20 split: 80% pointing out what we do right and do well; 20% pointing out our weaknesses. However, 100% of the conversation should focus on growth and reassurance, because that is what God commands us to do.

"Therefore encourage one another and build each other up, just as in fact you are doing." (1 Thessalonians 5:11, NIV)

Today, commit to being a springboard of encouragement.

I will build up others.

My Reflections

After reading today's note, I realize

_____

_____

_____

_____

_____

The key point or phrase I want to remember and practice today is

_____

_____

_____

_____

_____

Today it was easy/difficult for me to experience joy when

_____

_____

_____

_____

> "Nothing limits achievement like small thinking; nothing expands possibilities like unleashed imagination."
>
> William Arthur Ward

I grew up in a small town of 716 people, but I learned a long time ago that my dreams don't have to be small, too. I love thinking big and shooting for the stars. Do I make it every time? Absolutely not, but I am farther along because I tried than if I had let excuses or fear hold me back.

What are your dreams? What is stopping you from pursuing them?

Real joy lies in pursuit, not necessarily in achievement. We've all been told, "Keep your eye on the prize." But, honestly, if we're always looking ten feet ahead, we might accidentally miss the log that is about to trip us, or we might neglect the beauty that surrounds us on the trail. Yes, we need to have the end in mind. But we need to pursue it one purposeful step at a time.

So let your dreams soar and know that with God the things we deem as *im*possible become "I'm possible."

Today, push through the stop signs and pursue your goals.

I will aim high and enjoy the pursuit.

My Reflections

After reading today's note, I realize

_____

_____

_____

_____

_____

The key point or phrase I want to remember and practice today is

_____

_____

_____

_____

_____

Today it was easy/difficult for me to experience joy when

_____

_____

_____

_____

"Joy is the settled assurance that God is in control of all the details of my life, the quiet confidence that ultimately everything is going to be all right, and the determined choice to praise God in every situation."

Kay Warren

You are now on Day 90 of experiencing joy in your life! Congratulations on taking steps to live with delight daily. Throughout this book, I shared what I absorbed along my journey of pursuing one single word: Joy is not just a feeling; joy is also an action. I found that I am able to choose delight no matter my circumstances, that God is in control of the events and that I am in control of my reactions.

That is what *I* learned. Now, I want to know what *you* discovered.

Today, answer these three questions:

How do you define joy? _____

How have you seen joy appear in your life?_____

How will you keep pursuing joy? _____

I will seek joy daily.

My Reflections

After reading today's note, I realize

_____

_____

_____

_____

_____

The key point or phrase I want to remember and practice today is

_____

_____

_____

_____

_____

Today it was easy/difficult for me to experience joy when

_____

_____

_____

_____

Final Thoughts

"My wish for you is joy. When you wish someone joy, you wish peace, love, prosperity, health, happiness … all the good things."

Maya Angelou

I want to thank you for going on this journey with me. I am excited to say that as the first ninety days come to a close, joy has taken root in my heart. I hope you can say the same. Remember, *joy is a choice*, and each time you make the decision to embrace this gift God has given you, yours will grow incrementally.

He continues to teach me more about finding delight. I look forward to sharing my newest discoveries so that, together, we can be refueled and renewed in spirit and mind.

I would love for you to explain how *you* are finding joy. Please feel free to share your experiences on my social media sites or email me at info@dawnkaiser.com.

May joy follow you all the days of your life.

With gratitude,

Dawn Kaiser

About the Author

An inspirational speaker and joy-refueler, Dawn Kaiser encourages others to unleash joy in their journeys.

Speaking at more than one hundred live events annually, Dawn is known for her inspirational ideas on leadership, joy, positive psychology, faith and much more. She delivers keynote speeches, seminars and virtual learning events using a heart-centered approach, engaging techniques and actionable content to energize, encourage and equip individuals and organizations to flourish.

Dawn is a University of Illinois—Urbana Champaign graduate who is a student of life and a teacher of living. She holds a B.A. in business and an M.A. in education. She is also a Certified Human Resource Professional (PHR) and SHRM–CP. When she is not traveling to speaking engagements, Dawn volunteers locally and globally, plans amazing adventures with her family and friends, and sips hot chocolate while searching for the next big *aha*! moment in a great book.

CPSIA information can be obtained
at www.ICGtesting.com
Printed in the USA
LVOW01s0845290716
497903LV00002B/5/P